The Self~Esteem Repair & Maintenance Manual

By
B. David Brooks, Ph.D.
Rex K. Dalby, M.S.

Edited by Paula J. Hunter

HOUSE

Book design, cover design and illustration by John Benson, Corona del Mar,
California.

Printed and bound in the United States of America.

Library of Congress Cataloging-in-Publication Data

Brooks, B. David, 1938 –
      The self-esteem repair & maintenance manual / by
      B. David Brooks, Rex K. Dalby; edited by Paula J. Hunter
      p. cm.
1. Self-respect. 2. Self-respect—Problems, exercises, etc.
I. Dalby, Rex K., 1948 – . II. Hunter, Paula J. III. Title.
BF697.5.S46B76   1989
158'. 1—dc20   89-36692

ISBN 0-943793-27-0

ATTENTION ORGANIZATIONS, INSTITUTIONS AND CORPORATIONS:
This book is available at a quantity discount on bulk purchases for use in
education, business, or sales promotion. For information contact our Special
Sales department at 714 646 6406.

To Dad and Mom,
who laid the foundation,
and Rosemarie who helped me
build upon it.

BDB

To Steve Pierson,
(with honorable mention to
Sydney and Lauren).

RKD

ACKNOWLEDGEMENTS

Thanks to those who shared ideas and gave input: Christy Gail Boettner, who offered a poem, Ambrosio Lopez-Hidalgo (*Life is a Tango Played by a Japanese Band*), and the members of the California Task Force to Promote Self-Esteem and Personal and Social Responsibility.

To those who have encouraged and supported me—Joanne McFann, Bernie and Colleen Brooks, Terry and Joyce Brooks, Donald Brooks and Laurie Brooks— a special acknowledgement.

To Eileen Brooks, Pat McCarthy, Clyde Thomas, Diane Gilbert and Laura Hobb, thanks for your encouragement. And to Paula Hunter, the deepest thanks. It is because of you that this project is a reality.

BDB

This book has been a true labor of love for me, and a dream come true. It is living proof that all we discuss within these pages is true. As they say, however, "I could never have done it alone."

I thank the following for their teachings and/or their never-ending support of me as I have grown both personally and professionally. They have all, in their own special ways, contributed to this book: my parents, my sister Cindy and my brother Dale, Natalie Bogin, David Brooks, Carolyn Dalby, Sheryl Jacobs, Mindy Littlejohn, Robin Park, Kathy Pierson, Whit Plummer, Karen Sawyer, Jerry Sconce, Trish Teleshuk, Harry Winters, Gina Sanchez, and, most of all, Paula Hunter, without whom this book wouldn't exist.

RKD

INTRODUCTION

You may be wondering how a book on repairing and maintaining your self-esteem can be under 150 pages long. Shouldn't it be 300 pages, or maybe even two or three volumes? Isn't this a very complicated psychological issue requiring deep study and analysis? Can I really repair and maintain my self-esteem with such a relatively short book as this?

The answer is a resounding **YES!** Since the release of our videotape entitled "Self-Esteem: Building a Strong Foundation for Your Child," one of the most frequent comments we hear is, "It's great to help our kids build their self-esteem, but what can I do for myself? What can I do when my self-esteem is low?" We are often asked if we know of a book that simply lays out an action plan, a guide with steps a person can take to feel better about himself or herself. What people tell us they are looking for is "...a book without a lot of theoretical discussion, psychological mumbo jumbo and six syllable words."

Out of these requests this book was born.

The premise of this book is something we might refer to as **"The Four A's": Attitude, Action, Achievement and Acknowledgement**. To assure the successful repair or maintenance of your self-esteem, you must have the right *attitude*, take the proper *action*, which will lead to *achievements*, and then you must *acknowledge* those achievements. When we say acknowledge, we're talking about congratulating yourself, which we'll discuss in Chapter One. We call this the *Success Cycle*. Our goal, indeed our promise, to you is to keep it simple and guide you in making these Four A's part of your daily life. Improved self-esteem will naturally follow like new grass after a rain.

This is a "how to" book; all you need to know is on these pages. You'll find **exercises** which will serve as mental calisthenics to prepare you for self-esteem repair or enhancement. We've inserted several meaningful and encouraging **quotations** which you may want to copy and post on your bathroom mirror or wherever you'll see them often, because every little suggestion that helps to cheer you on is important. And at-a-glance **recaps** periodically through the book will emphasize very clearly the significant points made along the way.

It should be noted right from the start that simply reading this book will not result in your feeling better about yourself. You must take **action** to make a difference in your life. Often people avoid taking action, looking instead for "magic wands" that can be waved over them, making their lives better...making their wishes come true.

In our experience, there are no magic wands. The magic is within you. Our intention is to guide you through a process that will help you discover that magic and put it into action to repair your self-esteem. Then, by following suggested maintenance techniques, you'll maintain your self-esteem at a high level—opening doors to new heights of happiness and contentment.

B. David Brooks
Rex K. Dalby
Long Beach, CA

TABLE OF CONTENTS

CHAPTER 1

Setting the Stage

ongratulations! You've just taken the first step toward repairing and maintaining your self-esteem. Be proud and congratulate yourself! Satisfaction and contentment as a result of your achievements, no matter how tiny, are a very important principle of this book. We'll be wanting you to congratulate and reward yourself often during your progress with us.

When we say congratulate and reward yourself, we're really talking about two different things. To congratulate yourself is to recognize and take pride in your achievements. We want you to do that after every success, no matter how small. To reward yourself is to treat yourself. When you have had a series of successes, take the time to do something for yourself. Go to your favorite restaurant, or buy that little something you've always wanted. Treat yourself in a special way—you deserve it. We hope you'll make a habit of such acknowledgement not only as you go through this book, but on through the rest of your life.

Throughout this book we'll seek to keep it simple—whether it be the language, the format, or the process itself. So we'll begin with a simple definition of self-esteem: Self-esteem is a way of feeling about yourself. If you accept and like yourself as you are, warts and all, you are said to have high self-esteem. If, on the other hand, you don't accept and like yourself, you are said to have low self-esteem. We believe it really is that simple.

Now, we realize you hear other terms used to describe these feelings about yourself. Those terms include self-image, self-perception and self-concept, and each of these terms has various definitions. We don't want to complicate the issue by constantly differentiating between these terms—they all pertain to your feelings about yourself. So, for the purposes of this book, we'll call the concept we're dealing with self-esteem.

As Rex recalls, "I attended a panel discussion recently in which two 'experts' spent several minutes of valuable time arguing over the difference between self-esteem and self-image. This time could have been more productively spent discussing the issue itself, which is what the audience really came to hear. The audience had no need for ivory tower arguments; they merely wanted to know what they could do to feel better about themselves."

There is another definition of self-esteem we especially like. Even though it is a bit more complicated than our previous definition, we feel it is worth covering. The California State Task Force to Promote Self-Esteem and Personal and Social Responsibility adopted this definition of self-esteem: "Self-esteem is appreciating my own worth and importance and having the character to be accountable for myself and to act responsibly toward others."

Let's look for a moment at the parts of this definition. First we have *appreciating my own worth and importance.* You have to understand that you are a worthy, loving person—that you are capable not only of giving to and appreciating others, but giving to yourself and appreciating yourself. The fact that you are here on the face of the earth means that you are important and

3

of value, so you must value yourself. Some might think this appreciation of self is automatic. It is not. It comes from practice; it comes from understanding your feelings, your perceptions, your attitudes, and *accepting* who you are, and it comes from recognizing that you *can* feel good about yourself, you *can* reward yourself, and you *can* consciously improve yourself.

The second part of the definition is *having the character to be accountable for myself.* When you take action, you can't be pointing toward someone else as the cause for that action. You must have the character and strength to understand that the actions you take are *your* actions and you are responsible for them. You are responsible for the way you behave, the way you fail to behave, and the way you either reward or chastise yourself for your successes and your failures. Accountability means understanding that you make deliberate choices, that you have the responsibility to act on your decisions, and to accept the consequences of those actions.

The third part of the definition is that you must *act responsibly toward others.* You don't live in a vacuum. Responsibility toward others doesn't mean that you have to (or even should) accept all that others say and all that others do. It does mean, however, that you have to be conscious of the fact that your behavior influences, and is influenced by, others around you. Your actions do have an effect upon those who love you, those who care about you, those who work with you and those who you encounter in your daily life, no matter how unimportant the contact might seem. This interaction must be considered in order to make responsible choices.

RECAP: Self-esteem means appreciating my own worth and importance, and having the character to be

accountable for myself and to act responsibly toward others.

Throughout this book, to illustrate some of our ideas, we'll use the metaphor of the automobile, likening it to the development of a human life. Think for a moment of the automobile as it comes off the assembly line. It's all shiny and beautiful, and in perfect working order. But once it's out of the factory, it can suffer a ding here or a dent there, or maybe even a serious breakdown.

If our automobile breaks down, we take it to an expert—to a mechanic who has the knowledge and skill and the tools necessary to fix what's wrong. We explain what symptoms the car is showing...imitating the strange noises it makes, illustrating the mushy brakes or the slipping transmission. The mechanic asks us questions, maybe performs diagnostic testing; then, to the best of his or her ability, determines what's wrong with the car.

At this point, we could continue to talk with the mechanic about what's wrong. We could even repeat this step weekly...or even daily. Talk, talk, talk! But obviously, just talking about what's wrong with the car won't fix it.

At some point, someone must take action.

So it is with human beings. When we need fixing, whether a little or a lot, we may choose to go to a therapist. We may tell this person how we feel; he or she will ask many questions, and, just like the automobile mechanic, the therapist will try to determine what's wrong. At this point we may continue to see the therapist every week and talk about our problems each session. You may know someone who has been seeing a therapist for a year or two or even longer. They go in religiously—once, even twice a week—and talk. Again, all that talk, talk, talk. They do this with the belief that this talking, in and of itself, will repair them. Often this belief is reinforced by the therapist.

It is our belief, when it comes to repairing self-esteem, that simply talking about it is not enough. Talk without *action* won't solve the problem. Please don't assume we're anti-counseling. We believe counseling is in many cases necessary and very valuable. But, when the problem is related to self-esteem, we firmly believe talking must be accompanied by *action*.

"Even if you're on the right track, you'll get run over if you just sit there."

—Will Rogers

Self-esteem is built by a step-by-step progression of successes, and successes are the result of action. Recall The Four A's from the Introduction: *Attitude* leads to *Action* leads to *Achievements* which, when *Acknowledged,* lead to *higher self-esteem.* Think back to some of your past achievements: getting an A on your math test, being complimented on a job well done, getting a job promotion, and so on. Recall how you felt at those moments of success. Wasn't it pure contentment and a sense of pride? It felt good! Achieving and maintaining that happy, satisfied feeling of success is what we're talking about.

Staying with our automobile metaphor, you may decide to read some books and fix the car yourself. Fine! You'll hopefully remember that nothing happens until action is taken—so you'll lift the hood and get started. Great! And when you work your way through to a solution, you'll feel better about yourself and more confident about fixing the next problem. (And you'll also have a fixed car.)

Insofar as your daily life is concerned, we'll show you how you can structure successes into your life—how to create for yourself a *Success Cycle* by performing tasks you know you'll perform well.

RECAP: Attitude leads to Action, which leads to Achievements which, when Acknowledged, lead to higher self-esteem.

This book will be of great value to you only if you follow through with action. We offer no magic wand with which you can instantly transform your life. We do, however, give you tools that will prove to be golden when "applied as directed."

When you do apply these tools as directed, you'll maintain a high level of self-esteem. If there is a breakdown, you'll be able to repair your self-esteem. And you very well may change your life if that's what you choose to do.

The tools are in your hands.

Embarking on Your Journey

CHAPTER 2

As you embark on your journey toward higher self-esteem, you must put yourself into the forefront of the matter. You must put your **Self** into self-esteem. To do this, you need to understand the elements from which self-esteem develops.

Where do your thoughts and feelings about your Self come from? We human beings differ significantly from other living creatures on this earth in that we build our concepts about our world from many different sources of input. These concepts result in feelings, attitudes, emotions, perceptions and expectations. We unconsciously gather this input and sift it through a mental filtering system—of which each human being has a unique version—eventually discarding some input and retaining some. It's important to remember that much of what is said and done around us leads to the development of concepts about ourselves, and that those concepts lead to behavior—the way we act.

Now you're probably asking, what does all this have to do with self-esteem? Well, once we realize that a major source of self-esteem is an accumulation of data—or input—which we react to, we can begin to see how the way we feel about ourselves and the way we interact with others is **learned**. That data which we *choose* to focus on, our successes for example, shapes our thinking. The word *choose* is used here intentionally because we, in fact, can and do decide what we think about, although sometimes the decision doesn't feel like a conscious one.

"All that a man achieves or all that he fails to achieve is the direct result of his own thoughts."

—James Allen

We are all literally bombarded by input from everywhere around us, though we remain unconscious of much of that input. To illustrate this, we like to use the analogy of the video camera. When you turn the camera on and train it on an object, it records what's there, or it receives "input." It records everything—the sounds and the pictures. Let's say you're on a trip to Mexico, and you videotape a beautiful village. Long afterward, when you pull out the tape and share it with your friends over salsa-flavored popcorn, you suddenly realize that there are sounds or dialogue you were not aware of while taping, because you were so busy doing the taping and concentrating on what you saw in the lens. Now that you have it on tape, you can choose to listen to and watch more than just the central object or theme you were concentrating on while doing the taping. You might notice that, in addition to the beautiful village, there is also a beautiful sunset in the picture. Or you might notice the litter in the street. You choose to notice what you want to notice. And so it is with input you receive all your life. While you're busy getting through each day, focusing intently on only certain aspects at a time, you may not be noticing much else of what's going on around you, be it good or bad, or whether it's having a positive or a negative influence on you. What's going on around you *is* influencing you just the same, much like the unnoticed details of the video influence the overall outcome of the taping of your trip.

Let's think about an automobile assembly line. When we're born we're pretty much like empty automobile frames, beginning the trip down the assembly line. As we move through our formative years and on through life, things get built onto (or into) this frame of ours. Some of the add-ons—like bad habits—we're better off without; others—like positive thoughts—we cannot do without if we are to be happy and successful. The point is, we can passively allow things to be added onto our "frames," or we can take control of the assembly line process and direct our own modification. If you are to repair and maintain your self-esteem, your first responsibility is to accept that you'll always be wearing two hats, so to speak. You should see yourself moving along the assembly line as well as controlling your progress on it.

As you think of yourself as the one in charge of the assembly line watching yourself move along, you begin to realize both of these truths: you have the power of choice, and you are the direct beneficiary of your choices. As the person in charge, you can choose to focus on the cheaper, less effective "parts" to fill out this frame (or ideas to place into your brain), or you can choose the highest quality parts and make a better model. It's your choice; you're the one with the power here, just as you are in your life. Let's look at the model you've already assembled.

Try this.

Exercise: In the space below make two lists. On the left list as many things as you can that you really don't like about yourself. On the right list those things that you do like about yourself.

Don't Like   Like

Which list is longer?
Which list was easier to write?
What items ("parts") would you choose to keep?
What items would you choose to change?
Are there things you'd like to eliminate?

Did you find it difficult or maybe even embarrassing to do the *Like* list? In our experience the vast majority of people who complete this exercise develop a *Don't Like* list much longer than their *Like* list. Also, in many cases, they report that the *Likes* were much more difficult to list than the *Don't Likes*. One reason the *Likes* are difficult to list is that many of us have been taught not to brag about ourselves. But the most important reason the *Don't Like* overshadows the *Like* list is, we often tend to focus on the negatives, not taking time to think about the positives. As a result, we're not even conscious of all the good things about ourselves. We don't even have those positive thoughts in mind to think about.

"When I work with people in individual counseling sessions," notes Rex, "I often ask them, 'What do you like about yourself? What's special about you?' The response in a large percentage of cases is, 'Nothing.' This is an example of people's strengths being entirely out of their consciousness."

The fact is, much of the input we accept and think about is less than complimentary. It may be downright degrading. If you are to maintain a high level of self-esteem, you must practice the skill of filtering out the bad, and concentrating on the good thoughts and positive input. Don't accept only the input coming to you from others; take control and purposely input your own positive thoughts. Put your Self into the process. It's okay to think about your strengths! When we say you can choose the high-quality parts to create the best "model" of you possible, we mean you should focus on the positives...or the *Likes*.

You'll recall that your first responsibility in repairing and maintaining your self-esteem at a high level is to see yourself moving along the "assembly line" of your development, as well as to acknowledge that you're the one in charge of controlling that assembly line. Now, your second key responsibility is to remember: *you are what you think*. The point here is that we human beings think in words. Sure, there are feelings and emotions and many shades of gray, but even these are influenced by the words we use—our personal language.

There's an expression we're fond of that's appropriate here: "You can't have the thoughts if you don't know the words." For example, if you've never heard the word *stupid*, it would be difficult for you to think of yourself as stupid. But if whenever you did something wrong, someone called you stupid, you might learn to believe you are stupid. Following along that line, if the words you say to yourself, in your head (as we all do, all the time), are positive and encouraging, you'll feel positive and encouraged. You'll have the thoughts, because they follow from the words.

Don't forget that your self-esteem is based on your definition of your Self...the words you use to define *you*. The more responsibility you take for the words which make up your thoughts—the more you put your Self in self-esteem—the greater your ability to repair, maintain or enhance your self-esteem.

RECAP: Two major sources of the thoughts we have about ourselves are what we hear and experience, and what we say to ourselves.

Let's be a little more specific about the sources of input from which we create self-esteem. The fact is that self-esteem comes from several sources as you move along the assembly line of life. When you're young, it comes mainly from your **family**. As we shall see, early family days have a great impact on your feelings of self-esteem.

In most families, when a child is born a great deal of attention is paid to almost every little thing the baby does. Parents will stand for hours at the foot of the crib waiting for the child to turn over. When the child finally turns over, they laugh and clap—"Oh look how wonderful our baby is!"—because the infant has made this progress. Of course the baby picks up on this celebration and, as much as an infant can, feels good about the success.

As we mature, we must realize that people often give mixed signals...and that even our parents and relatives can be inconsistent in the messages and signals, subtle or direct, that they give us. We must learn to carefully evaluate those signals, always giving ourselves the benefit of the doubt.

For example: parents and other family members often say things to each other, in anger or otherwise, that they don't really mean. If mom says to little Jenny, "You idiot! You'll never learn," Jenny probably won't be able to understand that Mom's just angry...she didn't really mean it. Rather, those words will probably go straight to Jenny's delicate little "input center." If these words are often repeated, she may begin to believe them. Or if older brother Johnny habitually refers to little brother Tommy as a "freak show reject," little Tommy could easily come to believe there's something wrong with him.

In many adults, self-esteem suffers greatly when the hurt from cruel or thoughtless things their parents or family members said to them is used as their basis for defining themselves. Unfortunately, those things that were said in anger seem to be so much more dramatic and impactful; therefore, they are more memorable, and may remain an influence for a lifetime.

The issue here is one of evaluating input and sorting through it—running it through that mental filtering system of ours. So where does self-esteem come from? It comes to a large degree from input received from other people, especially from our families.

A second major influence in the development of self-esteem is **interaction at school.** Children who are successful at school, who feel good about themselves and who develop into successful, productive, responsible adults, generally had positive interactions at school. They've been helped to overcome their weaknesses, and they've learned to identify their strengths.

School teachers, of course, have a tremendous influence over children. Their language, be it positive and supportive, or negative and degrading, directly affects not only the learning of the students, but also their developing self-esteem. When kids are helped to feel good about their successes, they feel better about themselves; consequently, they develop the skills and confidence they need to succeed.

In addition to input from teachers, some of the most influential input kids receive is from their peers. It's so discouraging to see children be cruel to each other. Teasing, taunting and ridiculing have a harmful effect on some children; these children often make the sad choice of carrying these words and thoughts as heavily burdensome excess baggage into their futures.

Take a minute to think back to your childhood. Is there some negative baggage you're still carrying around? Maybe you're still bruised by always being the last one picked for teams ("My grandmother could play better than a retard like you!"). Maybe you were teased about your clothes ("I've seen bums dress better than you, ya rag picker!")...your complexion ("What girl would ever kiss a geek like you?")...even your conscientiousness ("Always kissin' up...what a nerd...."). You *can* rid yourself of that bad-news-blues baggage, you know—get it right out of your mind. Mentally discard that damaging negative input: Picture yourself at the airport, any airport (or train station...whatever image you like; you're the creator of this picture), lugging that excess baggage. Then mentally put it down and walk away, telling yourself, "I'm rid of all that unpleasant stuff." You might even go so far as to visualize putting it in a locker, then throwing away the key. If it comes back to your mind, shake it away. Refuse it. Keep reminding yourself, "I got rid of that nonsense for good."

You're the only one who can keep a thought or feeling or image alive. If people have called you a klutz all your life, and you've learned to call yourself a klutz, you've *accepted* this criticism. That means you're allowing other people's words to control your perceptions of yourself, and, therefore, to control your life. Every time you become aware of thinking, "What a klutz I am," force that thought out of your mind by saying, "I am coordinated, I can handle whatever I set my mind to, and anyone who thinks otherwise is totally wrong."

"Take charge of your thoughts.
You can do what you will with them."

—Plato

We've discussed the influence of family and school and how they affect our images of ourselves. Another major influence we must always keep in mind is that of **society in general**. The media (films and television in particular), popular music, churches, and organizations such as Little League, Girl Scouts and Boy Scouts, and Girls and Boys clubs, all play a part in influencing us. When you *choose the good* in these influences, experiences and involvements, your self-esteem can be enhanced.

On the other hand, when you choose to associate with and be influenced by non-supportive, unaccepting, uncaring elements of society, your self-esteem will be diminished by the barrage of negative input from those sources. The thought of accepting the negative input of society brings to mind a term used in the computer industry: garbage in, garbage out. Allowing the ills of society, the garbage, into your life, results in getting equally foul consequences from your life. Your success in repairing and maintaining your self-esteem is affected by the influences you submit yourself to, and your acceptance or rejection of the input they provide.

RECAP: We gain self-esteem or lack it as a result of input received throughout our early years from parents, relatives, teachers, peers and others. As we get older, we can choose to accept or reject the input; we can let it destroy our self-esteem, or build it.

This brings us to the final influence upon your self-esteem, which is probably the most important and powerful of all. **YOU!**

Your influence on yourself is largely an issue of language. For our purposes, language means the words you hear from others, the words you say out loud and to yourself, and all the other signs, symbols and gestures from your environment. At some point, as you grow, the input comes not only from external sources, but from internal sources as well. In other words, you begin to give yourself messages, commonly referred to as **self-talk**. If much of what you have focused on from the external sources has been negative, there is a good chance that your self-talk will be negative. If, on the other hand, you have focused on the positive, there's a good chance your self-talk will be positive.

"Think you can or think you can't; either way you'll be right."

—Henry Ford

The language you use with yourself, in your mind, shapes your self-concept, then, ultimately, your behavior. It's vital that you understand the critical part your language plays in determining how well you maintain a high level of self-esteem. For example, when someone criticizes you, your self-talk might be, "They're right, I'm a jerk." But understand that you could as easily respond with, "Hey, that's just that person's opinion. I know what he thinks of me isn't true."

Think for a moment about your self-talk. Have you ever made a simple little mistake, the kind all human beings make from time to time, and heard yourself say, "I'm so dumb! I can't do anything right!" It's sad how common this type of personal language is. The truth is you can do lots of things right, and do so many times during the course of each day. It's amazing that negative self-talk seems so easy a trap to fall into. Why is it that, when we do things right, we don't seem so inclined to say, "I'm so smart! I do so many things well!"

David explains encountering a teacher whose job was to interview hundreds of teachers for career tracking purposes. "One of the questions she asked was, 'What would you say if you gave a test and all your students got 100%?' She told me that all their responses were along these lines: 'The test must have been too easy'; 'I used the test last year, so the kids knew what to expect'; or, 'The kids must have cheated.' She went on to say that not once did a teacher say, 'I must have done a great job of teaching.'"

Keep in mind that the bad or good feelings you have about yourself come from the thoughts you bring along with you...the language you carry around in your head.

Since we've established that self esteem is so strongly influenced by the input that you accept from others, both past and present, it seems to follow that to build self-esteem you must go through a long and difficult analysis of your past. Right? Well, as far as we're concerned, no, that's not right. We can't emphasize too strongly that your past is just that: *past.* It is gone, it's done, it's behind you. To return to our automobile metaphor, don't concentrate on the rear view mirror, but, rather on the windshield and all that lies beyond it. Keep your eyes on the road! Concentrate on where you are and where you're going, not where you've been.

Certainly there are some very important things to consider from your past. You can't change them; try to acknowledge and learn from those things, correct and adjust their negative impact as you can, and move along. Past occurances must be far from the central theme of your thinking if you are to repair, maintain or enhance your self-esteem. Accept that you are living in the here and now. Decide right now, at this very moment, that your thinking will center on now and on the future. Yesterday is beyond your control, but you can do whatever you want to about today and tomorrow.

RECAP: The past is past. Embark on your journey to success now, at this very moment.

A last critical aspect of self-esteem we must consider is **temporary mood swings**. No one feels really good and is bursting buttons with high self-esteem all the time. No one can possibly be up every minute.

In all honesty, there are some things you just don't do very well. We all have strengths and we all have weaknesses. But when you attempt to tackle one of those areas at which you're not so hot *when you're feeling less than your best*, you may be setting yourself up for failure. If you have to perform a task at which you're not so adept when you don't feel self-confident, lighten up! Give yourself a break, and congratulate yourself for giving it a try.

A good idea to promote success in repairing and maintaining your self-esteem is this: try looking at your life in segments. You may feel wonderful at home, have a good and fruitful personal life and be successful in meeting your responsibilities to your family, yet you get down on yourself because your achievement at work is less than you'd like it to be. This is when you can and should *compartmentalize*. Rather than allowing a lack of success in one area to spill over and begin to taint an area in which you're doing well, feel good about successess at home while you work on greater success on the job. Understand that in different areas of life you have greater or lesser capabilities and effectiveness. Isolate the areas in which you want to improve, and work on those without jeopardizing areas you feel good about.

David recalls such a case. "I once spoke with a person who had a self-esteem problem which was the result of her inability to read. She could read, but not very well. When she was feeling bad about herself, she'd grab a book, usually way above her level, and attempt to read it. Of course she experienced immediate failure, which confirmed her negative feelings about herself. She was creating a cycle of low self-esteem by taking action that reinforced her feeling of low self-esteem.

"I asked her to identify times when she felt good about herself, and accept that those are the times she should practice improving her reading skills. It was during this period that she could meet her failures and work through them, building upon her strengths. The mistakes she made didn't feel so devastating when she was feeling good about herself.

"She was encouraged to 'read up' when she felt up to the task. She was guided to go a little above her level of reading, and to tackle large chunks of reading material, like the entire newspaper, and then, most importantly, to congratulate herself for her success. She eventually began to talk about things she had read in the paper, and learned to tell herself, "I can talk about this intelligently because I read about it." This translated into better feelings about herself, which led to her attempting to read material that was increasingly difficult. The gradual improvement of her reading level and her thinking positively about herself led to a very pleasing Success Cycle which ultimately led to higher self-esteem."

RECAP: When you're feeling particularly low is the wrong time to focus on an area in which you're not having much success. It's the time to consider what it is that you do well. Focus on your successes and you'll begin to feel good again.

Language~ Discovering the Power of Self~Talk

CHAPTER 3

Picture a beautiful park. You're walking through the park, and you come upon a playground. Off to the right you see a slide. Remember playing on such a slide—your fingers clutching the railing at the top when you were too young to know if it would really be safe to let go? In this chapter, we're going to discuss slides, but not the playground kind. We'll offer an overview of how self-esteem can "slide" right on down to nothing.

As we mentioned in the last chapter, we don't believe it's necessary to spend years analyzing your childhood in order to feel better about yourself. We do find value, however, in understanding how certain events and thoughts in our lives lead to other events and thoughts. Understanding leads to control. By controlling our thinking, we can control our future.

We've discussed some aspects of life which impact self-esteem. In Chapter Two we introduced the concept of personal language. Let's be more specific and look at the importance of language in relation to what we call the Self-Esteem Slide. We've seen that if we choose to accept the negative input which can be found all around us, the result may well be negative self-talk (personal language). That negative self-talk may lead to self-doubt. Self-doubt is normal and is something we all encounter from time to time, but we must emphasize that run-away self-doubt can be destructive.

A person with self-doubt is not the person who says, "I'm a loser. I'll never amount to anything." That's a person who's given up. As we see it, people with self-doubt are just beginning to question their self-worth. They'll say to themselves, "Gee, maybe I am a loser, maybe I won't ever amount to anything," and so on. Again, we all suffer from self-doubt from time to time—it's quite common.

We've all had the experience of waking up in the morning feeling kind of down, or with "the blahs." But these feelings don't usually stay around for very long. They may last until that afternoon, perhaps even until the next day, but soon we're back to our old chipper selves. For others, however, self-doubt can be the beginning of what we see as the downward slide of self-esteem. If we allow self-doubt to germinate and eventually to dominate our thinking, we may end up at the bottom of the Slide.

RECAP: What you say to yourself—your personal language—is what you believe, and what you believe is who you are.

Let's start at the top of the Self-Esteem Slide. There you are a happy baby, standing on a nice, firm foundation of **high self-esteem**. You try anything, believing you can *do* anything, and you enjoy your successes. At some point, however, you begin to develop **self-doubt**. If you aren't careful and don't take control of your thoughts, you may slide right into the habit of not even trying. Your personal language will be something like: "Why bother to ask for a raise? I wouldn't get

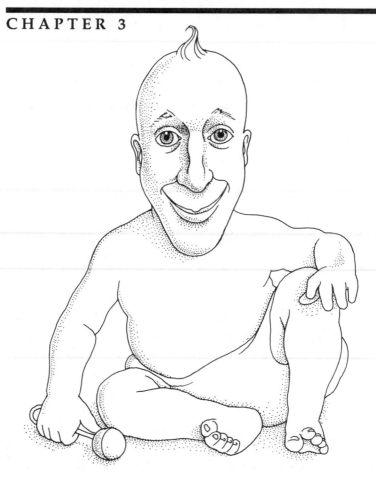

one anyway"; or on a larger scale, "Why waste my time applying for that job—there's too much competition. Besides, I'm horrible at interviews anyway." So you **don't even try**.

"This brings to mind a little saying I'd like to share," says Rex. "I heard it many years ago, and it remains very meaningful to me: 'Sometimes you have to reach out to the ends of the branches, 'cuz that's where the fruit is.' This saying gives me a mental picture of a huge tree, the biggest tree I can imagine. Hanging all over the branches of that tree is everything desirable in life...hanging right there for the picking. Also in this picture is a guy who has shinnied up the trunk of the tree, but he's not willing to reach out for all the goodies on the branches. He won't reach out—not even with one hand—for the fruit which would enrich his life. Why? You're right: he might fall. Many refer to this as *fear of failure*. So he spends his entire life hanging onto the trunk of that tree. Is he happy? Not really. But he's safe, and after while he kind of gets used to it, so it's not so bad."

How many people live their lives clinging to their own tree trunk when right there, within reach, is all they could ever want? We all know people who stay in jobs or relationships, for example, for ten, twenty or thirty years, when they know those situations aren't fulfilling or satisfying to them. "But hey," they'll say, "it's secure, and after all it's only 8 to 5. Besides, I've got great benefits." This is a graphic illustration of step three on the self-esteem slide—not trying. Many of these people end up in their later years regretting much of their lives. They wonder: "What if? What if I would have tried? Maybe, just maybe, I could have...." What a sad epitaph for a person.

"Of all sad words of tongue or pen,
The saddest are these: 'It might have been!'"

—John Greenleaf Whittier

We have all had things in our lives that we wanted to do, but, for many different reasons, didn't even try. We frequently hear from people who tell us they would like to change jobs but are afraid to. They usually have extensive reasons, more honestly known as excuses or rationalizations, as to why they don't try for the new job. Other people tell us about various areas of personal growth they would like to pursue, like being a public speaker, having a new relationship, trying a new sport...but they don't pursue those challenges, even though they believe they would be highly fulfilling. You might want to make your own list of things you've wanted to pursue but, for whatever excuses or rationalizations, haven't.

We are not saying that you should quit your job tomorrow and jump into a new field without proper preparation. We *are* saying that most of us can think of things we wish we would have done, but didn't even try. Often the reason for not trying is self-doubt, brought about by negative self-talk. Maybe the missed opportunity wasn't something as major as a job change. Many of us can remember wanting to date someone in high school or college but never asking, for fear of rejection. Does that strike a familiar note? (And we still wonder, don't we?)

Exercise: Think of some things you wanted to do when you were younger but never tried. What are some of the reasons you didn't try?

Now make a list of some of the things you want for your future but which you are not actively pursuing. List the reasons you are not trying for them. Be honest—no flimsy rationalizations.

A vital point in avoiding the early stages of the Self-Esteem Slide—**self doubt** and **not trying**—is this fact: it is not only *okay* to fail, but it is *necessary* to fail in order to be successful. No matter how you define success, no successful person exists who hasn't experienced failure along the way. In fact, we don't even like the word failure; we prefer to call them temporary setbacks, and view them as stepping stones.

A most impactful example of this fact is a chronology of the life of President Abraham Lincoln. He of course is known to every schoolchild in America as the man who held our nation together during the greatest threat to freedom in our history...a man of unfathomable strength and success. Rarely told are the great failures he experienced.

He is said to have written, "I am the most miserable man living. Whether I shall be better I cannot tell." And it is little wonder: In 1822, as a young man, he lost his job as a store clerk, and then was refused admission to law school due to lack of prerequisite education. He then entered into a business partnership, only to have his partner die, leaving him serious debts that would take him seventeen years to pay off. In 1832 he was defeated for the State Legislature. The next year saw yet another business failure. In '35, his long-standing female friend refused his proposal of marriage, and another former girlfriend's death left him bereft and heartbroken. He was defeated for Speaker in 1838, defeated for the elector in 1840, defeated for Congress in 1843, and, on the third try, elected to Congress in 1846. Two years later, at 39 years of age, he failed to get reelected.

His personal life and its tragedies are legend: the death of his beloved son Willie, a sadly empty marriage to the deeply troubled Mary Todd, whose difficult family caused frequent political embarrassment, a nervous breakdown...which was followed in a year by failure to secure an appointment to the U.S. Land Office. At age 45, Mr. Lincoln was badly defeated for a seat in the U.S. Senate; two years later, in 1856, he was named Vice Presidential candidate, but his ticket was defeated. In 1858 he again was badly defeated for the U.S. Senate. But, after perservering tribulations seemingly beyond human endurance, he was elected President of the United States at the age of 51.

Abraham Lincoln's road to becoming one of our nation's most profoundly successful leaders was paved with relentless failures; he endured and found greatness nonetheless. You'll hear many successful people echo the sentiment, "The only failure is in refusing to take risks." Paired with that fact, we cannot overemphasize the reality that to *experience* a failure is not to *be* a failure. Repeat that to yourself; believe it and take it to heart.

If we had experienced self-doubt when we were babies, we probably wouldn't be able to do half of what we do today. Take walking for example. Can you imagine a little baby thinking "Gee, that looks pretty tough. I'd probably fall and hurt myself. I think I'll just stick to crawling." Of course not! They get up, take a step or two, and fall down. And then they say "To heck with it, I knew I couldn't do it. I'm not going to try that again," right? No way! They take a few steps, fall down, take a few steps, fall down and continue to do so until they learn how to walk. The same is true for bicycle riding, swimming and countless other things we do.

"Only those who dare to fail greatly can ever achieve greatly."

—Robert F. Kennedy

Whenever there is something you want to do and you don't even try, you are giving up on *you*, and *you* pay the price. Not your parents, not your spouse, not your friends, not your colleagues, not anyone else. *You!* Giving up on yourself is learned. Back to the baby-learning-to-walk example: Babies don't give up. As adults we must unlearn the habit of giving up. Will you be rejected sometimes? Yes. Will you fail sometimes? Absolutely. But every failure brings you that much closer to success. And, rather than focusing on the failure, you can congratulate yourself for trying, get back up, and try again.

Suppose that you decide to go ahead and pursue an opportunity, self-doubt and all. Congratulate yourself for that decision! However, you must be very careful that your self-doubt doesn't sabatoge your efforts. For example, suppose there is a job you hear about for which you decide to apply. But you apply for that job with this attitude: "Well, I'll go ahead and try, but I don't think I'll get it. I mean, there are probably a hundred other applicants more qualified, but I'll try. And I'm scared to death of interviews, so I'll probably never get past the interview anyway. But, yeah. Sure. I'll try. But, I don't know, I don't think I have much of a chance." But...but...but.... And so on.

With that attitude, that language, how do you think you'll do? Probably not very well. When we let that negative attitude dominate, we generally get poor results. Remember the power of your language, your self-talk. In order to begin to increase your self-esteem, you *must* eliminate negative self-talk. We often hear people tell us: "I can't help it, I automatically think negative thoughts. That's just the way I was raised." One part of that statement is correct; for many people the negative thinking *has* become automatic, it *has* become a habit. But habits can be changed. Easily? No, of course not. We do not mean to say that any of this is easy. But all of it can be achieved if you have the right attitude and take the right action. And when you do take that action, the rewards are immeasurable.

"If you think you are a second class citizen, you are."

—Ted Turner

To eliminate negative self-talk, you first must be aware of when you are doing it. Be aware of your thoughts. Often negative thoughts pop up when you have made a simple mistake, such as tripping: "I'm so clumsy!" Or after responding wrongly to a question: "I'm so stupid!" and so on. So beware and be *aware* of such thoughts. When they present themselves, you must stop them. As we often tell kids: "If your self-talk is 'I can't, I can't, I can't,' you'll probably be right. If your self-talk is 'I can, I can, I can,' you will probably be right. The choice is yours."

Exercise: List some of the negative statements people make to themselves. Then rephrase the statement in a positive way. For example, "I am stupid" / "I am smart."

This will give you practice at reversing negative self-talk.

Let's see how this downhill slide can continue. As we have said, if you start with self-doubt, then attempt something while using negative self-talk, you will probably not do very well. Often, at this point, your doubts are confirmed. It is no longer "Maybe I'm stupid." Now it's "Boy am I stupid!" And you get a

distorted image of yourself. This distorted image results in your saying things like: "I'm just plain worthless." This, of course, is distorted, because no one is
worthless. We each have strengths, talents, and abilities
that are unique to us. At this point, however, you may
have lost sight of any good that exists within you. You
begin to focus on the negatives: "My life's going no-
where, I'm a loser, I'll never amount to anything...I'm
worthless." If asked why you feel that way, you are
quick to point out, "I tried, but I failed, like I figured I
would." Your mistakes and your failures, which we all
have as human beings, are used to "prove" that you are
a "loser."

In addition to developing a distorted image of
ourselves, we begin to get an erroneous picture of
others. We begin to compare ourselves to others and, in
most cases, we lose. "I'm no good, but look at them.
They've got it made. They're good looking, have lots of
friends, a happy family, good job. Boy, they don't have
any problems." Of course this is erroneous, for, as we all
know, no one goes through life without problems. So
don't play the comparison game.

If the Self-Esteem Slide stopped here life would
be bad enough. However, let's carry this scenario out to
its extreme and see how serious the results of low self-
esteem can become. Our world today is filled with
many serious problems: apathy, depression, drug and
alcohol abuse, suicide, and many other personal ills. If
we look at the third step down the Slide, **distorted self
image**, we can see that it is just a short distance to these
problems, which signify the absolute **bottom** of the
Slide.

It is important to understand many of these
problems are really just short-term solutions to pain. If
I feel like I'm a loser, a worthless human being, and it

will never change, why not use drugs? Many people know first hand that drugs and alcohol are great pain relievers. Suicide is the ultimate pain reliever. Now, we don't mean to say that these are appropriate solutions, because they certainly are not, under any circumstances. But perhaps you can get a sense of how easy it could become to rationalize these things to yourself and end up at the bottom of the Slide, amongst all the garbage.

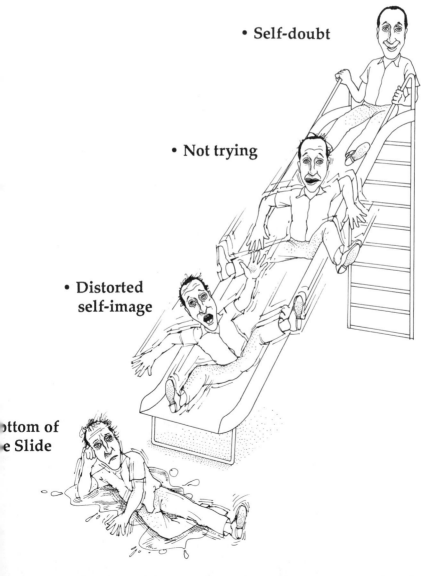

• Self-doubt

• Not trying

• Distorted self-image

ttom of e Slide

CHAPTER 3

That our concept of the Self-Esteem Slide is likened to a playground slide is no accident. When sliding down a playground slide you often feel out of control, especially as you build up speed toward the bottom. The fact is, you aren't out of control at all. At any point along the way down, you can grab the guard rails, push your legs into the sides and slow yourself down, or even stop yourself completely. If you want to, you can even work hard and climb right back up that slide. We believe it is the same with the Self-Esteem Slide. It often feels like our lives are out of control, like we are sliding right on down, unable to stop ourselves. Just as was the case with the playground slide, this is not true with the self-esteem slide either. You can always "grab the guard rails" and take control of your life.

In order to stop that downward momentum when you find yourself on the Self-Esteem Slide, you must have a firm hold on your attitudes and your actions. We've been sharing the idea that your language leads to certain attitudes and assumptions about yourself, and those attitudes and assumptions lead to behavior. You have control of your language, your self-talk, and the input you accept from your environment. Consciously reject the negatives and accentuate the positives. A strong, positive attitude will always serve as an effective guard rail, allowing you to reverse any downward momentum and work yourself back to the top.

RECAP: Take control of your attitude and actions; they determine where you are on the Self-Esteem Slide.

Framework for Success

CHAPTER 4

At this point we should take a moment to review the underlying philosophy of this book. You'll recall from the Introduction that the key to building self-esteem and feeling better about yourself is The Four A's: the right *attitude*, taking the right *action*, leading to *achievements*, and then *acknowledging* those achievements. That is the premise of this book.

Now, we don't mean that you should take action without some sort of a plan. To do so would greatly enhance your chance for failure, thereby resulting in lower self-esteem. Conversely, the more prepared you are, the greater your chances for success and higher self-esteem.

For the next five chapters we'll give you a framework, complete with tools and instructions—like any good repair manual—for taking action and attaining success in repairing your self-esteem. We'll follow in Chapter Ten with the framework to help you maintain your self-esteem at a high level.

It's no accident that this book consists of ten chapters whose titles, using the first letters only, spell out S E L F - E S T E E M. That may help keep you on course.

These instructions work equally well whether your goal is big (starting your own business) or small (building your vocabulary). The process is the same. We will take you through this process by way of questions you should think about and answer.

So let's get going!

CHAPTER 5

Envision

If you could have *anything* right now, what would it be? A new job? A new house? A yacht? An airplane? Better health? A larger vocabulary? A loving relationship? All of the above? The first tool in your self-esteem toolbox for constructing the life you want is **envisioning:** seeing in your mind a picture of what or where you want to be. In this chapter we'll concentrate on helping you determine what it is you want in life.

Don't worry about the how-to's, the logistics, the seeming impossibility, the supposed impracticality, or "what people will think." Those will be answered later. The fact is, in order to achieve your goals, you first must know what they are and where you are going with them. As says the caterpillar who encounters a confused Alice at a crossroads in Lewis G. Carroll's *Through the Looking Glass,* "If you don't know where you're going, it doesn't matter much which way you go."

All changes in life begin with someone's envisioning beyond the moment...beyond "how it's been done up to now." Think about it. In manufacturing, in art and music, all medical breakthroughs, advances in computer technology and automotive design, adjustments in how our schools teach our children, new products on grocery shelves, each new motion picture, television program, record or book—all are the results of envisioning. Other words used for envisioning are imagining, picturing, visualizing, future thinking, or that overused phrase, goal setting. Sometimes we call it dreaming.

In this chapter we're asking you to become a dreamer. Throw out all those negative words and limitations and go back to being that little boy or little girl who thought he or she could have, do or be anything. Free yourself for dreaming.

Let's think about dreams. Remember when you were a child and you had all of those magnificent dreams? You believed you could do anything. You were going to be an actor and a firefighter and ride the rodeo and have a hundred-foot boat and....well, we could go on forever, because in your mind you could...and did. Often the younger a person is, the more vivid and outlandish or outrageous his or her dreams are. Even in their play, kids get fully into character for whatever they're imagining...making peculiar noises and comical faces to make their "just pretending" real. What a blessing to know no inner impediments to freedom of activity and expression...which we adults know as inhibitions.

Children have the ability to dream freely because they don't place limits on their dreams, and they don't weigh their dreams down with judgmental attitudes and nay-saying. As they get older, however, children hear things like, "Don't be such a dreamer," and "Be more realistic." It's almost as if, as we mature, an automatic braking system kicks in. It's a tragedy of life that for many people, dreams become limited with age, and phrases like: "I can't do it," or, "It'll never work out for me," or "Who do I think I am, anyhow?" begin to creep into their heads. In many cases, as people get older, this defeatist self-talk increases and eventually they put their dreams aside completely. Somewhere along the line, dreaming is given up. Dreams just stop.

"Hold fast to your dreams, for if dreams die, then life is like a broken winged bird that cannot fly."

—Langston Hughes

It's important to understand that dreams are free. There are no limitations to them, and no one can take them away unless you allow them to. A very meaningful example of this concept lies in the story of Victor Frankl. He's an internationally renowned psychiatrist who endured years of horrifying treatment in Nazi concentration camps. His writings indicate that while locked up in an agonizingly hopeless situation, his survival was due to the fact that he would not allow his merciless captors to take away his thoughts, his dreams or his vision of the world. He is a man who is fond of quoting the famous philosopher Nietzsche: "He who has a *why* to live can bear with almost any *how*."

Let's look at some ideas that will help you in this process we call envisioning. By the way, don't get tied into these concepts as if they were steps that have to be done in a particular order or manner—like assembly-required toys at Christmastime—or even like a typical repair manual. These are hints which can help you be more productive or successful at envisioning. Taken altogether or in part, in any order, these suggestions serve as a starting place, and mark the path to a happier, more fulfilled you.

We'll take you through the ESTEEM chapters as

promised, by posing some questions. These will lead you through the process for building the skills that are the basis for high self-esteem. Here we go.

QUESTIONS FOR ENVISIONING:

When am I best able to think?

Find a time of day or night when you are comfortable, when it's quiet, when there are few distractions, and when you can freely think and envision without interruption. You may find that morning is the best time for your envisioning; many people do. Maybe you'll find a comfortable slot at noontime, or perhaps at night, when all is calm and quiet. (Be careful if you do envisioning at night or when you are tired, as you might find yourself doing the other kind of dreaming after you've fallen asleep.)

Find the time you are most comfortable *and* most alert, and choose that for your envisioning time. Also keep in mind that dreams, ideas, and goals can hit you at any time. When they do, jot them down, to be expanded upon later at a planned envisioning time.

Where is the best place for me to envision?

Find a place in which you are comfortable, and in which you enjoy being. This doesn't mean you have to get into your car and drive an hour or two to somebody's condo at the desert, or cabin in the mountains or to the beach. It happens that the beach is our first choice for our own envisioning, with the soothing sounds of the surf drowning out all distractions. But for you it could be under a tree in your backyard, or in your living room or basement or on your patio or porch. Find the place that works for you. It will be your regular place for envisioning.

David recalls a friend's envisioning place. "One person I know found that when he really needed to think—to look to the future and begin to develop plans and strategies for his life—his "place" was in his car, parked on the hillside, overlooking the city. This freed him from worries and other distractions, especially the telephone, and enabled him to practice envisioning." Find your own place that's easily accessible, comfortable, pleasant, and with as few distractions as possible.

What should my thought process be?

Make this a *conscious* process. Be aware of the fact that you are controlling your thoughts. You are deliberately looking into the future. This is not simply daydreaming. You might want to actually talk to yourself as if you are two people. Get a conversation going; for example, think of two voices, one on your left, one on your right, but both of them *your* voice. The voice on your left asks, "What is it you really want?" The one on the right answers, "A new job." Suppose the left side says: "You don't have the training for a new job." The right might say, "No negative talk! I can get the training! I'll find the training!" and so on. This practice of carrying on a two-way conversation within yourself is one way to make your envisioning a conscious, controlled process, not just random daydreaming.

Unless it makes you feel silly, there's no harm in doing this dialoguing aloud. This may make the process more real. Another way to keep the process conscious is to take notes while you're envisioning.

Am I being negative in my thinking?

All negative words must be eliminated from your vocabulary during this time. Words and phrases like *don't, won't, can't, never, no way,* and *it's impossible* must be deleted from your vocabulary while you're envisioning. This is not the place to put restraints, restrictions or limitations on your thinking. True, you do have to deal with reality, but that comes later. Envisioning should allow you to dream the greatest dream without crushing that dream with thoughts like, "I can't do it," "It'll never fly," "Who am I kidding," or "Nothing will happen, I'll just disappoint myself."

Keep a positive point of view. Envision things you want to gain, not things you want to get rid of. Practice envisioning things you want to have and do and be. Suppose one of your goals is to lose twenty pounds. Your envisioning shouldn't be about how heavy you are or about how much weight you want to lose in a month, a year or any given period of time. Your envisioning should be about your target weight and the good that will come when you reach that weight...how you'll look and feel when you have reached your goal...the great clothes you'll be able to wear...and the proud feelings you'll have about your achievement.

The secret to the envisioning process, again, is to look into the future. At this point don't concentrate on specific strategies for accomplishing the goals, but look at how you will be, what you will have, and what it will be like when you've achieved what you've dreamed about.

Am I thinking for myself?

Make these *your* dreams. Though you sometimes might wish you could, you cannot dream for someone else. Your friend who badly needs a new car or your parents who greatly deserve a trip to Hawaii are certainly worthy of dreams, but you can't bring their dreams to reality. Now, if your goal is to buy your friend a new car, or send your folks on the trip, that's great. But if your dream is for them to be able to afford the car or the trip themselves, it won't work. That's out of your control.

Of course, the accomplishment of your dreams may affect others. For example, when the things you envision begin to take place, you'll have a different frame of mind, and others will see and react to you differently. Maybe by example you'll encourage them to envision for themselves. Just remember to make yourself the focus of your envisioning rather than focusing on your hopes for someone else. You can't change anyone else's life—to think you can is to kid yourself. But your own life is yours to mold however you will.

Also remember that someone else's dream for you doesn't necessarily have to be your dream. We frequently hear from people who have suppressed their own dreams and done all they could to bring to reality the dream someone else had for them, only to meet with disappointment. You've surely known examples of this, like those who enter a particular profession because that's what their fathers wanted for them, or those who marry a particular person because that's what made their mothers happy. People who end up living their lives to suit others' dreams won't ever be completely happy and fulfilled. They must dream their own dreams, and live for themselves.

RECAP: Your dreams must be conscious, positive and for yourself.

As you envision, you may find negative thoughts and limitations creeping in and pushing your dreams right out of your mind. The first step toward the solution of that problem is the realization that you cannot think two thoughts at the same time. For example, say you're in a meeting and the person directing the meeting says, "Be thinking about next Saturday's function while we go through the slate of officers for next term." The slate of officers is announced and discussed and analyzed; then the director says, "Okay, what have you come up with for Saturday?" Obviously, if you were paying attention to the discussion of the slate of officers, you had no time to consider options for Saturday's function, and have to answer, "Nothing yet...I've been a little preoccupied." You may get the official scowl, but no one who understands how people think would ever ask you to think two thoughts at once.

Your thoughts are either here or there; they can't be in two places at the same time. If negative thoughts and limitations begin to creep into your mind, take control and push them right out. Replace them with your positive thoughts.

If you're sitting in a comfortable place envisioning your future, thinking about the way things are, the way things will be when you reach your goal, and you find yourself saying, "Yes, but..." or, "Oh, I couldn't do that," or, "I'll never accomplish that," consciously say to yourself, "I am envisioning the future. I am eliminating all thoughts not directly applying in a positive way to the area of my life I'm envisioning." Then repeat over and over again those words which affirm what you're envisioning. "I am thin. I am successful. I have many friends. I have a good job. I am happy. I am prosperous."

As you affirm these positive statements, you'll

51

find that you're accomplishing two very important things: you're allowing your firm and positive visions to sink more and more deeply into your conscious mind as realities, and you're preventing limitations or other negatives from entering your mind.

RECAP: Limitations on your visions or dreams may slip into your envisioning. Consciously push those limitations out of your mind, and affirm as though your dreams are already realities.

Remember earlier in this chapter our mentioning the special ability of children to dream freely, without limitations? Try to recall when you were a kid, and practiced that talent often. Let's try to get back to that honest, open, hopeful, childlike frame of mind. To help you think as freely as you did as a child, without limitations, try this.

Exercise: Imagine you have just stumbled upon a wierd little magic lamp, like in the movies or fairytales. You rub it (because that's what they always did in the stories) and, sure enough, your genie appears (in chartreuse harem pants, purple shoes with turned-up toes, and a bejeweled black velvet vest). But this genie is much more savvy than the old bald ones in the movies. He doesn't want you putting limitations on your wishes. So he doesn't just give you three wishes; rather, he tells you that you have fifteen seconds to write down in the space on page 54 everything you want. He tells you that whatever is on the page at the end of the fifteen seconds is yours. As you can imagine, if you open your mind and think freely you'll get many more items on the page. Just let it flow! If you start to question and doubt, to edit and correct, you'll find less on the page. Seriously, we're asking you to take fifteen seconds and put as many of your wishes and dreams as possible on the page. If possible, have someone else time you so you are not distracted by checking the clock. For goodness sake don't cheat yourself out of a fraction of a second! These are your wishes and dreams!

MY DREAM LIST

What you have just done is practiced envisioning, with free flowing thought, without restrictions. The reality is, of course, that there are no genies who, with their *abracadabras*, make wishes come true. But envisioning can and will set you on the path to making those wishes come true. The point of this exercise is to have you practice envisioning without limitations. If you found it difficult, it may be because you allowed the limitations to control your thinking without even realizing it. Dreaming is a natural human tendency. But we're so practiced, so skilled at being "safe," setting up safety valves so we won't be disappointed, and letting doubts and limitations creep into our thinking, that we often don't give this natural dreaming process a chance.

In the next chapter we'll look at how you can take those wishes and dreams you envision and turn them into reality.

ACTION STEP ONE: Envisioning

Take yourself through the envisioning process and pick one dream for yourself. Write the dream with today's date and when you want to achieve it—in a week, a month, a year, five years, or whatever you decide—in the space below.

Today's date:

Dream:

Date I will achieve my dream:

Now, for completing your first Action Step toward achieving higher self-esteem, congratulate and reward yourself. *Take pride in your achievement.*

CHAPTER 6

Strategize

Now that you have an idea of what you want, it's time for your next step: **strategizing**. Millions of people stay in the dreaming stage and never advance to the action stage; consequently, they never fulfill those dreams. But when you do what we prescribe in this book—providing all the action required—you are well on your way to fulfilling your dreams...and building your self-esteem.

Can you imagine an NFL coach beginning a Super Bowl without a *game plan?* General George S. Patton advancing on the enemy without a *battle plan?* Or on a more day-to-day basis, a teacher trying to teach first graders to read without a *lesson plan?*

"Men never plan to be failures; they simply fail to plan to be successful."

—William A. Ward

Game plan, battle plan, and lesson plan are all terms we use for *strategies*. In fact, the word strategy originally comes from the Greek word for *general*. (In

Funk & Wagnell's New Comprehensive Dictionary, strategy is defined as "The science and art of conducting a military campaign by the combination and employment of means on a broad scale for gaining advantage in war; generalship.") Of course we're not saying you should run your life like a war, or act like a general; we're simply saying you need to have a plan of action.

Let's start turning your dreams into realities. A very important part of the process of bringing dreams to life involves making those dreams more specific. The first step here is a simple one: change the label from dream to **goal**. The word *goal* is much more powerful and dynamic than the word *dream*. We'll discuss goals more thoroughly later in this chapter, but for now remember, what you want is no longer in dream form. It's a goal. This differentiation is important.

Think back for a moment to the automobile we spoke of in Chapter One. The car doesn't just appear at the end of the assembly line. Extensive planning (strategizing), sometimes for years, precedes that journey along the assembly line, so the automobiles finally manufactured are the best they can be, and so they're produced in the most cost-effective, efficient manner possible. It's the same with goals and plans for accomplishing them. Now that you are beginning to define your goals, you have to take the time to strategize, to look at where you are, at what you need to do to reach your goals, and when you want to get there. Remember to keep your goals in front of you—both mentally and in writing—as you work through this chapter.

By no means do we mean to imply that everything you ever dream needs to be objectified, worked on, strategized and strived for. Of course some dreams are just enjoyable musings...little pleasurable fantasies that should and always will stay in that form.

RECAP: Before taking action you must have a plan, or a strategy.

QUESTIONS FOR STRATEGIZING:

What is my goal?

Earlier we asked you to relabel your dreams as goals. The dream you wrote at the end of Chapter Five is now a goal. Use that goal as your working goal for the remainder of this book.

Is my goal reachable?

This is a question you must answer carefully. For example, if you are forty years old and want to be an NFL quarterback, that may not be a reachable goal. However, if you are forty years old and would like to be an airline pilot, that may be reachable (although many people might tell you it's not).

"You may think this is an unrealistic example," says Rex, "but I have a friend, Ron Snedecor, who was first hired as an airline pilot at age forty." The point is, you must be careful not to rule out a goal too quickly without having thoroughly investigated all of the possibilities. Grandma Moses didn't begin to paint until she was in her eighties, and twenty-five percent of her paintings were painted after she was one hundred years old.

What is necessary to achieve this goal?

This question involves looking at what is commonly referred to as "the big picture." Think back to our metaphor of videotaping in Chapter Two. The big picture includes all those tiny details you were unaware of when you focused on one small portion of what was around you. Now you need to look at the details. Determine objectively what you'll need to acquire your specific goal. For example, if your goal is to own a big screen TV, it helps to know what different types are made, what features are and aren't important for you, who manufactures big screens, where they're sold, what kind of guarantees are offered, what the price range is, and so on.

If your goal is to open a shoe store, you need to know about city, state or federal requirements, permits and licenses, how to contact the manufacturers representatives and how to purchase inventory from them, what kind of fixtures will be required to properly display shoes in your store, who, what and where your competition is, how to find a viable location for your store, and on and on.

If your goal is a new job or career and you've settled on what it will be, you need to find out the educational requirements, work experience necessary, what companies offer that position, where they're located, and so forth. You get the picture.

When do I want to accomplish my goal?

Based on the information you discovered as a result of the last question, you must now set a realistic time for when you want to acquire or achieve this goal. It's not enough to say "I want to climb Mt. Everest some day." Think of time in specific terms, because there's no such thing as "someday." At least it's never been on any calendar we've ever seen.

Here is where you need to be realistic. Suppose you have always dreamed of being a mountain climber. You attend a motivational seminar where the speaker enthusiastically tells you, "You can do anything you put your mind to!" You leave the seminar all pumped up, and you decide you are going pursue your dream. Of course you're not going into this half-heartedly...you're ready! You set a goal that you are going to climb Mt. Everest one month from today.

The reality is that you've never climbed so much as an anthill, but that's okay; after all, that guy said you can do anything you put your mind to. In truth, you're setting yourself up for failure. You may go ahead and try to climb Mt. Everest next month, but more than likely you would fail (if you don't die first). And then you'd probably say to yourself, "I knew I couldn't do it." You would end up feeling worse about yourself than before you tried.

The same goal with a different time line might be realistic. For example, a goal of climbing Mt. Everest in three years could be reachable, assuming you do all the training and preparation necessary in the meantime.

You may have no desire to climb mountains, but hopefully you'll always have a personal "Mt. Everest" challenging you, whether it be changing careers, finding a fulfilling new relationship, writing a book, or whatever really gets your juices flowing. It's important to keep in mind our previous caution that many, many people stop at the dreaming stage. Setting the time line for when you want to attain your goal is another part of the process of moving from goals to achievements.

What are the obstacles to achieving my goal?

Whenever you set out to achieve a goal, you're going to find some snags along the way. For example, suppose you decide you want to get a better paying job. You wisely do some basic research and determine that the position you're aiming for requires some schooling. However, you discover that the schooling that would qualify you for this employment is available only at night school, and you work from three o'clock to midnight on the job you have now.

The reality is that your current position is an obstacle, standing in the way of your advancement. You must now strategize a way to overcome that obstacle. Do you quit your job? Do you change your work hours? Do you seek out other training?

An example of an obstacle that's not always apparent is a friend or family member. Sometimes there are subtle barriers put in front of you by a misguided person or people who have unconscious fears of your success or happiness. For instance, you may know of a person who has set a goal to lose weight, only to be sabotaged by other members of the family who are jealous because they aren't successful with weight loss themselves.

Other possible obstacles include insufficient education as in our example above, lack of money, lack of transportation, inadequate resources, lack of support and encouragement, lack of accessible information, and so on.

Where am I now?

What attitudes, skills, aptitudes, and tools do you possess *now* that will help get you what you want? This is the time to take inventory of yourself—making note of all the attributes and talents you have that will help you toward achieving your goal.

What personal qualities will get you closer to your goals? For example, if your goal is to meet new people and broaden your circle of friends, what are the beneficial traits you have *now* that will help you make more friends? Maybe you have a winning smile, or a genuine interest in other people. Perhaps you're an especially good listener. You might have an unusual past, or an exotic hobby that people you meet would enjoy learning about.

From a more tangible point of view, if you want to start a gardening service, list the equipment you already have—from mower to blower to truck to haul debris. If you want to set yourself up as a mechanic, look at your skills as well as your tool kit, noting what skills and tools you already possess to do the job you want to do.

The purpose is to identify every possible advantage you have going for you at this moment. *Identify your strengths!* Remember the *Likes* list from Chapter Two? Here we see all the more clearly, and more from a practical point of view, how vital it is to focus on the positives.

You may know of a singer-songwriter named Phoebe Snow. Her story is a good example of identifying strengths and focusing on those positive elements and characteristics. In 1974, her career was very high-profile and successful with the release of *Poetry Man*. A series of difficulties and setbacks caused a long hiatus from her work, but, as a testimony to her newfound belief in her strengths, her work and herself, she released a highly acclaimed album entitled *Something Real*. Ms Snow is quoted as saying, "If I've learned anything, it's that no matter where you work or what you do—no matter what industry or what job—if you have a very positive and firm self-image, you'll make it. And that's what I'm working on, right here and right now." (*Los Angeles Times*.) She had the right attitude, identified and believed in her strengths, and perservered.

By taking inventory of yourself, you'll not only be able to identify what you need to learn or acquire to accomplish your goals, you'll also have the important benefit of focusing on your strengths right from the start. You'll begin the process toward achieving your goals feeling better about yourself, so you'll have an important head start.

What do I need to do or acquire to reach my goal?

Now that you've taken inventory of what you currently possess, you must determine what you need to develop or acquire to reach your goal. Referring to the preceding examples, what are the shortcomings which make it difficult for you to make new friends? Maybe you're judgmental, or too lazy, or too serious, or too complaining. What problems would you encounter as a gardener? Maybe you'd need to learn how to solicit new clients. Or, as a mechanic, maybe you work at a very slow pace, and would have difficulty finishing jobs to suit your customers' needs until you learned to work faster.

On a more simplistic level, suppose you want to go on a Carribean vacation. What are some of the things you'd need to do to prepare? You'd need to determine the best season to travel in that part of the world, to talk to your boss about getting the time off work, and to check into travel packages, hotels, flight schedules, whether you'd need a visa, a passport, etc. Some of the things you may need to acquire are: Money to pay for your time in the sun, appropriate clothes, perhaps

SCUBA gear, a good sunscreen, maybe an internationally-accepted credit card...and so on.

For another example, let's go back to your goal to climb Mt. Everest. You've wised up a bit, and set a time line of three years for making the climb. What must you do in the meantime? You start by researching what training and tools you need, then you go about obtaining them.

What are the intermediate steps necessary to achieve my goal?

Seldom can you reach a goal without taking intermediate steps. These steps become mini goals in and of themselves, and can be very rewarding along the way. Every time you accomplish one, pat yourself on the back.

Suppose it's Monday and you're having a big dinner party on Saturday. What intermediate steps do you need to take? First you must plan the menu. Then, because you know you can't cook everything the day of the party, you plan to prepare some items ahead of time. On Thursday morning you might do the shopping. On Thursday evening you could prepare a dessert that can be frozen. On Friday you prepare the hors d'oeuvres platter that can be refrigerated and then baked on Saturday. Each of these intermediate steps toward ensuring the success of your dinner party on Saturday evening is essential for your acheivement of that goal.

Regarding the goal to climb Mt. Everest, you set an intermediate goal of climbing one of the local foothills. A realistic time line, enabling you to get the training and equipment you need, might be a month. So you decide that one month from today you're going to climb that hill.

When you accomplish that goal, two things will result. One is that you will be physically stronger. Two is that you will be mentally stronger. You will say to yourself, "Wow! I did it! If I can do this one, I know I can do a bigger hill next." And you find the next largest hill, being careful not to take on more than you can handle.

As we said earlier, mountain climbing may not be your cup of dehydrated soup, and that's certainly okay. The point is, whatever looms ahead as your greatest goal—starting a business, finding a better job, traveling, getting an education, or whatever—take it in steps, as discussed below, setting realistic time lines for each step.

It's the same with more complicated life goals. To achieve almost any goal you ever set, small or large, intermediate steps come into play. One of those news stories that all the nation's media rallied around provides a good example. It is the story of a paraplegic man named Mark Wellman, who had lost the use of his legs in a mountain climbing accident. In spite of this profound loss, he still dreamed of climbing new mountains. On such a quest, after eight days of using only his muscular arms (the result of extensive training) to pull himself up six inches at a time, Wellman and his fellow climber Mike Corbett (who climbed ahead to anchor ropes at each stage of the ascent) reached the summit of 3,500 foot El Capitan, one of the longest unbroken pieces of solid granite in the world, in Yosemite National Park, California. "You have a dream and you know the only way that dream is going to happen is if you just do it— even if it's six inches at a time," Wellman told reporters before beginning the grueling feat. (*Los Angeles Times.*)

Following Wellman's thoughts about dreaming, Corbett said when he was a kid, he would get in trouble for daydreaming and drawing pictures of mountains in his schoolbooks. After climbing El Capitan, he now says, "I'll never think I'm a bad guy for dreaming again." (*Fresno Bee.*)

You may want to review the dreaming process discussed in the Envision chapter, Chapter Five.

A little closer to sea level and a bit less dizzying but no less reassuring is the story of a newspaper reporter who dreamed of writing a novel. Author Robert Ferrigno, whose incomplete first novel earned him a heady $150,000 advance from his publisher, found encouragement from a novelist who he had interviewed as a reporter in Southern California. The inspiration came, says Ferrigno, when the best-selling novelist Elmore Leonard "really demystified the process...for me. His attitude was that you do it every day for X number of hours and at the end of the year you've got a book. It got me feeling that writing a novel was not a superhuman task; it was a human task." (*Los Angeles Times.*)

There is an infinite number of stories like these, and it's always wise to make note of them. Just as those strivers in the stories must, remember that whenever you perservere and take your goal step by step—even if it's just having the foresight to prepare for your dinner party in do-able steps so you can be the charming host and enjoy your own party—congratulate yourself for that perserverance, for that foresight. Recognize your intermediate steps and reward yourself for achieving them.

Now that you have an idea of the kinds of questions you must answer when strategizing, let's look at a few other important points. It's imperative that you put your goals down in writing. In the last chapter we had you *envision*, to get an idea of what you want. Earlier in this chapter we had you relabel that dream as a goal. Now we want to begin to make it even more concrete. You've probably heard much about goal setting and the importance of committing those goals to paper, in ink. We are often asked "Why do I have to write down my goals ? I know what I want, isn't that enough?"

Think of it this way: Can you imagine the captain of a freighter leaving a major port, bound for another country, saying, "Why do I need to plan and write down on paper how to get where we are going? I know where I want to go." Or a pilot not filing a flight plan? Or Mike Ditka, Don Schula, Tony La Russa or Pat Reilly not drawing up a game plan? You know very well there's a great chance that the freighter or the airplane would get lost. And the ball teams would probably lose.

We realize there are reasons that people don't write their goals, but none is very convincing. Some of the reasons we hear from people are:

1. "It takes too much time."
2. "I don't know what goals to write."
3. "I'm afraid if I write them down and don't accomplish them I'll feel bad."
4. "I don't know how to write goals."
5. "It doesn't really matter; as long as I think about them I'll be able to achieve them."
6. "Someone might see them and laugh."

Let's face it, the world out there can be pretty negative. Hundreds of different circumstances can cause you to forget about your goals, even if your intentions are the best. However, the more a goal is on your mind, the more likely it is that you'll be able to stay on track, especially in the beginning stages of your journey. Goals can be exciting and very motivating, but only if you're conscious of them. That's what many people—especially athletes—call *focusing*. Think back to the example of the meeting in Chapter Five, in which you were asked to be thinking about the Saturday event and that meeting's agenda at the same time. Remember you can't possibly do justice to two thoughts at the same time. One or both will suffer.

Almost everyone has living proof that our brains can firmly grasp only one thought at a time. Most of us have been put on hold on the telephone, listened to the music or been otherwise distracted, and forgotten who we were calling. There are few of us who haven't suffered the embarrassment of setting an appointment (or a date) with someone and, knowing how important is was, were just sure we wouldn't need to write it down in our calendar book. But, of course, we got distracted by something or other and forgot the appointment; therefore, we ended up appearing rude and thoughtless, when our sincere goal was to make a strong, positive impression. Even having a true brainstorm, in which you find the perfect solution to a nagging problem—so great you're sure you'll remember it forever—is no assurance the idea will stay in your head long enough to act upon it. So, the more you keep your goal in the forefront of your mind, the greater the probability you'll be working toward it.

Suppose one of your goals is to own a beautiful sailboat. You've gone to the boat shows, to the boat dealers, and have picked out the exact boat you want. The more that sailboat is on your mind, the more excited you will be and the more likely it is you will get it. You decide not to bother writing it down because, after all, you know what you want. It seems like that boat is all you can think about! But the next workday you have nothing but problems...just one of those days you wish you could have "phoned it in." When you get home you're tired and just want to recuperate from the rough day at work. Since you were so busy, you really didn't have time to think about the sailboat. As a matter of fact, if you are like most people, you probably forgot about it completely. Eventually the excitement, the actual stimulus of seeing that boat in your mind, begins to fade into the sunset...and so does your goal of owning that boat.

If a specific sailboat is your goal, you must keep thoughts about it literally in front of you. Hopefully you've put the goal in writing in the form of an affirmation. But you can't just write it down and stick the paper in a drawer, never to be seen again. We recommend posting that goal somewhere you'll see it many times during the day. There are lots of places you might do this: your bathroom mirror, at your work station—like on the telephone or some other such focal point, on the refrigerator, on the sun visor of your car, and so forth. This keeps you aware of and focused on your goal, and it has a motivating effect.

In addition to writing your goals, it is even more effective if you have an actual photograph of your goal or one that reminds you of it. Get the brochure of the boat you want and stick that picture up prominently in one or more of the places previously mentioned. A picture can remind you, excite you, motivate you and keep you on track. The point is, once again, you must do everything possible to keep that goal in the forefront of your mind. Keeping your goal before you also makes it a little easier to get through the daily problems we encounter in life. When it seems you "just can't take it any more," focus on that gorgeous picture of "your" boat or whatever it is you seek, and it'll give you renewed vigor to perservere.

More reasons for writing down your goals are:

1. It will be easier to clarify your thinking and organize your efforts.
2. You'll be able to check "at a glance" to evaluate your progress.
3. You'll have the opportunity to see your goals in relation to your time lines and adjust the goal or the time line as indicated.
4. You can check them off as you attain them. What a great feeling! Aha!...success! This little thrill of victory serves to further enhance your self-esteem.

RECAP: Goals must be achievable, and written with a realistic time line.

As you strategize, keep in mind the importance of taking baby steps toward your goal. If you were to take a class to learn French, you wouldn't walk out the first day fluently spewing monologues sounding like Louis XIV. You'd learn *bon jour, mon ami; como tallez vous?; merci boucoup* and maybe *parle vous Français?* After a while you'd put those words into sentences. Eventually you'd be communicating in that language.

When you think about the process of learning to speak a foreign language, you notice the ability occurs in small steps. It's a cumulative procedure—increasing by successive additions. Repairing and maintaining self-esteem is also cumulative. You build on each of your successes and thereby form a strong foundation of self-esteem.

---

*"A journey of a thousand leagues
begins with a single step."*

—Lao-tzu

In Chapter Five we said that your envisioning process was not the time to be "realistic." When you begin to strategize, or make definite plans for achieving the goals you have written, is the time to consider reality. Many times when talking to young people, we hear them report that they want to be a star athlete in the NBA or the NFL or in Major League Baseball. When we ask, "What are your plans? How are you going to get there?" they say, "Well, when I get out of high school I'll go to a major college and then get drafted." And they fully believe that. When asked what they're doing to make sure they get their diplomas and gain admission into the proper college, they don't have any idea. College prep courses? SAT tests? Checking college requirements? Funding assistance or scholarships? They know nothing of the process, and they don't have a sound plan (if they have a plan at all). Very few of these kids realize that out of the thousands and thousands of athletes that do get to college and do make the team—even if they have successful college careers—a very small percentage of them makes the pros.

Of course we're not saying you shouldn't set your sights on what you want for yourself and go for it. The point is, if you're going to set goals and strive to achieve them, you need a strategy...you need a plan.

Look into the future and be realistic about your goals. Is it possible for a young man to achieve a goal of playing in the NFL if he isn't planning to go to college and play football?   Can a young woman expect to make the Olympic Team if she's not in a long-term training program and competing at the college level?   In an extremely limited number of cases, the answer is yes. It's true that once in a great while we hear of a walk-on making an NFL or Major League Baseball team, or an incredibly gifted individual being spotted and taken under wing by a world-class coach or trainer. But it's an extremely rare exception.   The reality is that achieving goals calls for careful planning.

ACTION STEP TWO: Strategizing

At the end of the Envision chapter, we had you write down a dream. We asked you in this chapter to label it a goal. Now we'll walk you through the steps discussed in this chapter to help you strategize and attain that goal.

1. Re-write your goal here:

2. Write a list of all of the things necessary to attain your goal. (You will probably need to do some research to complete this.)

3. Being realistic, when do you think you can attain this goal? Write the date here:

4. List all of obstacles you can think of that may get in the way of achieving your goal.

5. List the things you have right now that will help you get there. (Attitudes, skills, tools, etc.)

6. What do you need to do or acquire in order to reach your goal?

7. Write down the intermediate steps you will take and when you'll accomplish them.

<u>Intermediate Steps</u>   <u>Date to be Accomplished</u>

Now, for completing your second Action Step toward achieving higher self-esteem, congratulate and reward yourself. *Take pride in your achievement.*

CHAPTER 7

Test

Y ou have envisioned your dream, turned the dream into a goal, and strategized a plan to achieve it. Now you're ready to *go for it!* No, wait a minute. The tendency for most people at this point is to act on their plans, but action now is a little premature. There is another step to the formula that can significantly increase your probability of succes. You know achievement (success) is what leads to higher self-esteem, so naturally you're going to give yourself every possible chance to be successful. So your next step is **testing**. "Test what?" you ask. Test your strategies, test your plans.

Expressions often used to illustrate testing are "Send out a feeler," "Send up a trial balloon," "See how the wind blows," or "Feel the pulse." As these sayings indicate, there are different ways to test. Testing can be training before you run the 10K, to see how much endurance you have. Or rehearsing before the curtain goes up, to check that you have your lines and cues right. Role playing is a way to test, and so is talking to people who have experience related to your goal.

Let's say your goal is to have a successful band. You don't just grab a group of people off the street, give them instruments and go out and get gigs. First you envision the kind of band you want. You decide what instruments are necessary for your kind of music, and then you audition people who play those particular instruments. Once you've found the people with whom you can form the kind of band you envision, you sit down as a group and **strategize**. One of the things you would do is decide on the songs you want to play, and what image you want to have. At this point you could say, "Okay, we've got our song list, we look good...let's go line up some jobs," and dive right into the **engage** process. We're sure you would agree, however, that before lining up jobs it would help to rehearse the songs, and maybe get feedback from people whose opinions you respect.

If you're new to sales and your goal is to be the top salesperson in your company, you first need the proper training. But beyond that, before you actually sit face to face with a real live customer, it is very helpful to role-play potential sales situations with someone in your office who's experienced in sales techniques.

What if your goal is to open a restaurant? A good way to test your strategy would be to talk to restaurant owners, managers, and chefs concerning menu planning, purchasing, profit margins, waste allowance, decor, kitchen layout, advertising and promotion, and such. It would certainly be wise to work for a while in the kind of establishment you want to open. Harry S. Truman's admonishment, "If you can't stand the heat, get out of the kitchen," might become very meaningful.

As you work through the test chapter you will find that strategizing and testing go hand in hand. When testing your strategies, you may need to adjust the plans you've made to meet the reality resulting from new information. That's one of the purposes of testing. Pat Reilly, the extremely successful coach of the NBA's Los Angeles Lakers, has been heard to say, "Game plans are great, but you have to be flexible enough to make adjustments."

RECAP: One way to help ensure success is to test your strategies.

QUESTIONS FOR TESTING:

Who are the best people to guide me, work with me, coach me and help me monitor myself in this endeavor?

The purpose here is only to identify people who can help you. These don't have to be people you know. It could be someone you saw at a seminar, an author of a book you like, someone who works in the field you're interested in, and so on. You must be *very careful* here. As we mentioned in Chapter Six, it can be a very negative world out there. When you ask for input or guidance from people you know—family and friends—some may be inclined to tell you, often in a seemingly caring way, all the reasons you won't succeed. Now, it's not that these people don't have your best interests at heart. Perhaps some may not, but the fact is that many of these people do care about you and your welfare. But they may bring their own personal set of problems and fears into the discussion without really knowing it.

Remember the tree we talked about in Chapter Three? We mentioned the people who cling to the trunk of the tree, afraid to reach for more in life. These are the people we're talking about here. They have long since quit dreaming, or taking any risks, and they transfer their own fears to you. They're concerned that in your reaching out for more in your life, you might fall. So they want to protect you. They'll tell you things like "There's too much competition in that field," or "You're too old to start that," or "You're too young to do that," or "Be realistic!"

Remembering some good advice he once received, Rex relates, "I once had someone tell me, 'Only listen to the people who are where you want to be.' It made good sense. If you think about it, many of these people who are trying to protect you are people who haven't had much success in their own lives. They are unhappy people. It's not that we can't or won't love them for who and what they are; but these are not the people we want to listen to when testing our strategies for achieving our goals. We want to listen to the people who are 'there,' who are doing what we want to be doing, who are positive, successful, and happy. We can learn from these people. We find that these people are usually willing to share what they've learned."

So be careful. Be fussy about the people you hang around with, whose input you allow into your mind. Now, you may ask, "Well, won't some people think I'm conceited?" Some might, that's true. But people who think like that certainly aren't considering your best interests. Your true friends, the people who really know and care about you, will understand. And they're the only ones who really count.

What if your goal were to improve your golf game? To whom would you go for help, the person who shoots 133 for eighteen holes, or the person who is consistently in the 80s? You'd go to the latter because he or she is where you want to be, doing what you want to be doing. Understand that very often the person who shoots 133 will try to give you lots of free advice, but we recommend that you take it for what it's worth (which is about what you pay for it). If your game is in the 200s you might want to listen to those 133 duffers, but if you're averaging in the 90s or low 100s, go to the person who's shooting in the 80s.

Often in sports—particularly in tennis or other individual sports—you'll be advised to "play up." If you choose opponents of your caliber or less, you won't learn and improve your game; instead, you'll begin to acquire their faulty skills and bad habits. Conversely, when you play up, you can learn the habits and skills of the better players and thereby improve your game.

We are often asked, "Where do I find these people?" The answer is, they are all around you. The yellow pages contain organizations and businesses that could be of help, like local Chambers of Commerce and business associations. You will also find them at classes and seminars, schools, colleges, and vocational schools, or churches, fraternal groups, and service clubs. They may be among your friends, neighbors, associates at work, or friends of friends. As you did when you were envisioning, let your imagination run wild.

Now that I've identified the people who are where I want to be, what do I do?

You've identified the people who can be of help to you; now, go to them and learn. One ingredient of successful interaction is assertiveness. (We caution you not to confuse assertiveness with aggressiveness; always maintain consideration and respect for the people from whom you're seeking input.) Contact these people and ask for their input. Be honest, open and candid. The worst thing they can do is turn you down, at which point you are no worse off than before.

If you encounter a potenially helpful person who's conducting a seminar or a class, don't be afraid to go up and make personal contact at a break or after the session. Most teachers, speakers or seminar presenters expect this, allow time for it—and usually are flattered by the interest. In fact, these people are often surrounded by individuals from their audiences, so be patient but determined. When you've been acknowledged, shake hands, introduce yourself and note how much you enjoyed and benefited from his or her presentation. Briefly mention your goal and ask if it would be possible to make an appointment for a short meeting at their convenience. Offer to take them to lunch. Give them your card if you have one, and get their card or whatever handouts are available with a phone number for the person, so you can follow up with a phone call.

If you don't have a business card, it's a good idea to have a very simple one printed with your name, address and phone number where you can receive business calls. Many quick print shops offer basic business card design and printing for around $25 or $30 for 500 cards, or watch for special offers. Your own calling card reflects your professional attitude, shows that you mean business, and helps you feel much closer to where you want to be when you achieve your goal.

If you can't arrange personal contact with a person you hope to meet with and learn from, telephone contact is fine, though it may be difficult to get through to someone who doesn't know you. Be businesslike, straightforward, friendly and, again, determined but respectful. If it's impossible to get through on the phone, a letter or a Fax would be appropriate.

Before your meeting, learn all you can about this man or woman. The more you know about them the more impressed (and flattered) they will be. If they have written a book, read it. Be knowledgeable about the company they own or work for. Do your homework! It pays off.

Don't arrive at your appointment ill-prepared or unprepared. One common trait of successful people is they hate to waste time. So be organized when you meet with them. Things to remember:

1. Be on time.
2. Respect their time.
3. Know what you are going to ask. Avoid impertinence.
4. Have your questions written down, but don't stick to your notes so much you don't key in on their responses and pursue areas they may bring up.
5. Thank them. Follow up with a thank you note.

We should point out, too, that there are helpful lessons to be learned all around you—and not necessarily from noted experts. Be aware of what's going on. Observe how people handle whatever business they're doing: if you want to be more effective at sales, notice the effective techniques used by store clerks, by telemarketers who call you, how even a young fast-food employee is trained to sell—suggesting additional items to your purchase, making you aware of special package deals or economies, but (hopefully) in a friendly, helpful manner. Or examine what was done wrongly. Note how characters in movies and on television conduct business. Observe what they do to promote trust, and how they create those win-win situations from which everybody benefits. And in all your personal interactions, be concsious of what tactics "work" on you, and which ones grate on your nerves. Consider the whole world your classroom.

Where can I go to practice or role play?

Envision situations where you might be able to practice. Be creative. If you are able, as with our friend who considered the restaurant business earlier in this chapter, to actually work in the area you're testing as a career move, such a hands-on test will be especially enlightening. Regarding our earlier example of becoming a top salesperson, one of the obvious places you can practice and role play is with fellow salespeople. (The successful ones!) If you don't have access to appropriate people, you might have friends or relatives who would be willing to pretend to be customers. Practice or role play with them, of course making sure they understand they must be serious and give you honest responses to your sales tactics.

Even role playing in front of a mirror may help—and we believe tape-recording yourself can be enlightening and constructive. What's important here is that you find some way or someone with whom to rehearse what you want to do. Each time you successfully rehearse something, that's another step in developing the confidence and skills that will ultimately result in your success and the raising of your self-esteem.

RECAP: **Effective testing includes practicing, role playing and networking.**

CHAPTER 7

Are my goals and time lines realistic?

An important determination during this testing step is whether or not the goals and strategies you've developed in the previous chapters are realistic. Do they work? Reaching beyond your grasp is essential to your progress, but you must be sure you can eventually get where you want to go.

As you gauge the do-ability of your goal, keep in mind the importance of achievable intermediate steps as well. You can test whether or not your goal is realistic by evaluating how well you are able to accomplish the intermediate steps. If you are unable to achieve the intermediate steps, it may be that your ultimate goal is too high. Maybe it's unrealistic, at least for now. If you are able to achieve the intermediate steps, but not within the time lines you established, it may be that you are expecting too much of yourself too soon. In this case, you'll need to adjust your time lines.

If you are honest with yourself and you determine that your goal or time line is unrealistic, don't discard it right away. Modify it. Suppose you are a beginning swimmer and you decide that by the end of the month you will swim fifty laps without stopping. You go to the pool to begin practicing and you realize, after completing one lap and feeling like you can hardly breathe, you're not in the condition you thought you were. It would be easy to decide to scrap the goal, but don't be too impulsive. Don't change your goal or time line yet. Congratulate yourself for the success you have had, and keep practicing. If after ten days you're only up to three laps, you need to reanalyze the goal and the time line. If you honestly decide you've put all you can into your swimming but you're not much closer to fifty consecutive laps, then perhaps you need to alter either

DONT QUIT UNTIL YOUR DEADLINE HAS COME, THEN RE-ASSESS

the goal, the strategy, or the time line.

How do I know when I'm ready?

Have you done everything you can to minimize potential failure? This is a tough question. You don't want to beat your head against the proverbial stone wall, but you don't want to give up too early. If you're completely honest, trust that you'll be able to make the right decision. What you don't want to do is stall.

Some people say things like "Well, I'm not quite ready," or "I need more preparation," or "You can't be too prepared, you know." As a result, some of those people never get started doing what they need to do to achieve their goals. They just spend their lives in a constant "getting ready" mode. So they never get anywhere.

"To reach the port...we must sail sometimes with the wind and sometimes against it—but we must sail, and not drift nor lie at anchor."
—Oliver Wendell Holmes

Of course you need to prepare, but don't use the need for more preparation as an excuse for not getting started. At some point you just have to say to yourself, "That's all the preparation I can do; now is the time." Most people know the point at which they are just making excuses because they are afraid to take that first step. Part of being a successful person is knowing yourself and being honest with yourself. Brought well to mind in the movie *The Dead Poet's Society* is the Latin term *carpe diem*: seize the day, seize the moment. When you have completed the Action Steps up to and including those in this chapter, you'll probably be about as ready as you'll ever be. When you know you've done all the preparation you can, go on ahead. Congratulate yourself for having gotten this far, and take the next Action Step.

ACTION STEP THREE: Testing

1. Rewrite your goal from Chapter Five here.

2. In the space below, start a list of people who can guide you, work with you, coach you and help you monitor yourself. You should be adding to this list constantly.

3. Begin to contact and make appointments to meet with or talk to the people listed above.

4. For each person you meet with, develop a list of questions you will ask them. Be sure you've learned all you can about them.

5. Congratulate and reward yourself
   for each success, no matter how
   small.

Now, for completing your third Action Step toward achieving higher self-esteem, congratulate and reward yourself. *Take pride in your achievement.*

CHAPTER 8

Engage

Now comes the part of the process which for many people is the toughest. But you've been gaining momentum all along the way, and you're ready! It's time to **engage** the gears and get that car rolling. Put your great goals and plans into action, bring together all you've learned, and make it happen.

Think back to the story about reaching out to the ends of the branches. Now is the time to make that big reach. An advertising slogan for Nike™ shoes says it all: Just do it.

Be enthusiastic! Now is not the time to be shy. You should by now have a clear picture of what you want, and a detailed plan for how you are going to get it. Now go forth with total confidence that what you've pictured for yourself is as good as yours—you just haven't taken possession yet.

"A man without enthusiasm
is like an automobile without gasoline."

—Anonymous

QUESTIONS FOR ENGAGING:

What do I do first?

Take the first step. There's a story about Napoleon pondering the *Champs Elysee* from his balcony in
Paris. He gathered his ministers and said, "I want trees
planted along this boulevard that will shade my troops."
One of his pragmatic ministers replied, "But general, if
you have those trees planted today, it will be a hundred
years before they will provide any shade for the sol-
diers." And Napoleon retorted, "In that case, you'd
better get started right away." Although Napoleon's
army never reaped the benefit of the shade, successive
armies, not to mention millions of tourists, have. The
point is, Napoleon knew someone had to take the first
step.

How can I avoid the dreaded "analysis paralysis"?

One of the things that stops people from engaging is what's called analysis paralysis. This obstruction
to progress occurs when we overanalyze our past, our
plans, our fears, our possible consequences, or anything
else pertaining to our situation. Repairing and maintaining high self-esteem is a process of thinking through
your options, possibilities, probabilities and consequences, but knowing when the thinking stops and the
action begins. Analysis has value in clarifying your
thinking and strategizing; however, it becomes a problem when the analysis itself becomes your only action
and you get stuck with your feet in a bucket. It's time to
move forward!

For example, suppose you want to go to dinner
with a friend. You call your friend to discuss (analyze)

where to go. First you discuss what kind of food you want. Well, you can choose from Chinese, American, Mexican, Italian, Japanese, Thai, Cajun, Korean, French and many others. Next, you debate what kind of atmosphere you feel like—someplace nice where you can dress up? Or someplace casual? Or perhaps fast food? Let's face it, this analysis can continue to the point where you want to just scream, "Forget it! I'll stay home and have a TV dinner." In the grips of such analysis paralysis, no one could ever make a choice from a menu anyhow.

That is one form of analysis paralysis. Many people avoid making decisions by continuing to list alternatives and possibilities. You could go on listing till you're blue-in-the-face, but at some point you must make a decision. That's the only way to avoid this form of analysis paralysis.

Another way analysis paralysis manifests itself is by compounding your fears. For example, the more you analyze what might go wrong, the more you may become convinced that it *will* go wrong. Suppose you're attracted to someone and would like to ask him or her out on a date. You could analyze all of the possibilities that can go wrong and say to yourself things like, "What if she says no? I'll feel so rejected. Or, what if she says yes and I get so tongue-tied I can't carry a conversation. Or what if I say something stupid and look like a fool, or what if, what if, what if...." See where it gets you? You've analyzed yourself right out of what may have been a great relationship.

By overanalyzing all that could go wrong, you begin to feel so afraid you never take the next step. You never even ask for the date. One way to counter the what-if? dilemma is not to ask yourself "What if he/she says no?" but rather to ask yourself "What if he/she says yes?" Focus on the positive. This takes us right back to the earlier part of this book where we discussed self-talk. Don't forget, your self-talk and your action are completely interconnected.

The answer to the question of how to avoid analysis paralysis is, practice being decisive, and focus on the positive if you're going to play the "what if" game.

How can I eliminate my fear and/or discomfort?

MASSIVE ACTION!

In most cases, you probably can't eliminate fear or discomfort completely, at least at first. But don't let that stop you from getting started. The only way to get over that fear and become more comfortable is by doing something and experiencing some success. Eliminating fear and discomfort creates a natural flow into building confidence and self-esteem.

Hopefully you will never become totally comfortable, because that would indicate you're no longer reaching. Once you reach a goal you should congratulate yourself, relax and enjoy what you have accomplished. That's good! Of course that's what we've been recommending all along. But remember there's no neutral in life: if you're not moving forward, you're slipping back. The tide is always either coming in or going out. Keep yourself sufficiently challenged to avoid a humdrum existence, and to keep that dynamism that makes life so stimulating. Hopefully you'll set your sights on the next plateau, and once again welcome back the butterflies. (Fun, isn't it?)

In our travels and our speaking engagements we frequently hear from people who would like to be public speakers themselves. But they admit to a certain amount of discomfort or anxiety when it is time to make a public address. After all, studies reveal that the number one fear of most people is, in fact, public speaking. And even people for whom public speaking is a goal sometimes find that fear won't go away. So what do we recommend when we are asked about how to overcome the fear and become good public speakers? *Public speaking!* As much and as often as you can. To any group that will listen. Practice leads to familiarity, and familiarity leads to comfort.

(A suggestion in regards to public speaking is, check out a public service organization called Toastmasters International, with chapters all over the world. Theirs is a program that is well thought-out and well implemented, and would probably be helpful to you.)

We realize that there are many different fears—fear of rejection, fear of failure, fear of success, fear of the unknown, and on and on. We do not wish to discuss them here because we feel nothing would be gained, much as we feel about overanalyzing your past. Your fears could have many different sources, and as many different labels, depending on who you talk to and to which school of thought they happen to subscribe. But don't get hamstrung over this issue. As we said, you can analyze anything, including fears, to the point that you are absolutely paralzyed. Fears are real. Refuse to let them get the best of you. Accept that you are going to feel some fear and discomfort, and take action anyway.

"Feel the fear and do it anyway."

—Susan Jeffers, Ph.D.

What should my self-talk be?

You'll recall earlier we talked about how important self-talk is. Your self-talk may be most critical at this stage of building your self-esteem. It may be the very thing that either prevents or makes possible your reaching out for what you want.

Programming your self-talk is valuable, and affirmations will help you do so. We alluded briefly to affirmations in Chapter Five as brief, positive statements of your dreams; now we'll examine them more closely as the excellent tools they are. An affirmation is a brief statement of the condition or objective that you want to achieve. It must be written in the first person, present tense, and the more specific the better. We can't overstress how vital it is that affirmations be expressed in the first person, *I*, and in the present tense, *now*. To affirm in the future tense, *will*, would be to verify in your mind that you haven't yet gotten to where you want to be, which could be self-defeating.

It's important that you have some general affirmations that you can repeat to yourself several times a day. Whenever you catch yourself thinking negatively, repeat your affirmations. A good general affirmation that a friend uses every morning when he wakes up, and then many times throughout the day, is: "I'm slim, trim, self-confident, happy and in great health." Do you see how such an inspiring statement of belief could start to sink into your mind? Again, this is an example of a *general* affirmation and is a good idea.

But you must also have some *specific* affirmations which pertain to the goals you are pursuing. Let's use the frequently-heard wish to be a slimmer, healthier, person weighing 120 pounds. The affirmation should not be "I'm going to lose weight. I'm going to start a diet tomorrow. I want to lose weight and I think I can lose weight, so I'm going to work real hard at it. I am going to be thin." That is all unfocused, unspecific someday kind of talk and, as you remember, someday never comes. The affirmation is, "I weigh 120 pounds." That's about as short and to the point as you can get. You might also want to have some "support" affirmations—things like: "I am thin." "I am strong." "I am healthy." "I am happy with myself."

We can't overemphasize the importance of affirmations. It's critical that you keep input we examined in Chapter Two, and the self-talk we discussed in Chapter Three, as positive as possible. One way of doing that is by using affirmations. The use of affirmations as you begin to take the next Action Step will help you avoid negative self-talk, build your confidence, and provide you with another way to keep your goal clearly in front of you. Soon your affirmations will become realities. As they do, your self-esteem will increase.

ACTION STEP FOUR: Engaging

1. Write your goal from Chapter Five as an affirmation.

2. *Get started!*

Now, for completing one more Action Step toward achieving higher self-esteem, congratulate and reward yourself. *Take pride in your achievement.* You're almost there!

CHAPTER 9

Evaluate

Y̶ou're in gear and well on the road to higher self-esteem. You can't just coast along, however. You must continually check your progress—**evaluate** where you are and where you are going. You'll need to periodically ask yourself whether your actions are getting you closer to or further from your goals.

As important as evaluation is, it is a step that's easy to overlook. Sometimes we don't evaluate because we forget. More often we fail to honestly evaluate because we don't want to face the possibility of failure. With the unfortunate tendency, as was discussed back in Chapter Two, to focus on our shortcomings or failures rather than on our progress and successes, perhaps it's a minor and subtle defense mechanism. Don't trick yourself. Honest evaluation requires acute examination, and hopefully it will reveal good, solid progress.

A current trend in training athletes, especially in individual sports like swimming, track and field, and golf, is to videotape their performances. Of course the athletes and their coaches and trainers don't just view the tapes for what's being done successfully and well; they pay particularly close attention to weaknesses and areas in which corrections need to be made. It would not do an aspiring athlete much good to ignore shortcomings. How could he or she ever improve? That's also true in your evaluation of your progress toward higher self-esteem. It's critical that you evaluate both your strengths and weaknesses so you can build upon your strengths and improve upon your weaknesses.

This is like the old question, is the cup half full or half empty? It's a matter of perception, of point of view. Let's go back to the Self-Esteem Slide for a moment. If you'll recall, people with low self-esteem often tend to have a distorted picture of themselves. They focus so intently on the negatives or failures that their negative perception of themselves becomes verified: they see themselves as worthless human beings, and they begin to act accordingly. Their self-esteem goes down the Slide to nothing.

For your evaluation process to be successful and productive, you must look at both the positives and the negatives in a balanced manner. As you discover areas of weakness, look at them from a positive perspective as being areas you can now learn from, and use that knowledge to correct your course.

Many people, if they evaluate at all, evaluate only their end results. It's not unusual for a person to only assess whether or not he or she was successful, and not examine the benchmarks along the way. Checking the progress along the way is equally if not more important than just critiquing the final results.

Evaluating the headway you're making is important for two reasons. The first is, if you're not evaluating your progress along the way, you may get off course. Once you are off course, the more time that passes, the further away you will get from your goals. It's easier to get back on course if you become aware of the problem before you've gone too far.

To illustrate, suppose you've achieved your goal of being the owner of a beautiful new sailboat. You're proud, and you're anxious to feel the wind in those sails. So you decide to sail from Long Beach, California, to Honolulu, Hawaii. You weigh anchor and sail out of the harbor, but, unbeknownst to you, you're ten degrees off course. Now, initially, ten degrees isn't that big a deal. If you had been evaluating your progress, you would have discovered the problem early on, so you could easily have corrected your heading. However, if you didn't discover and correct for that mistake, but rather continued on the wrong course, you would miss Honolulu by hundreds of miles.

Get the picture? As you see, the further you travel without correction, the further you will get from your goal and the longer it will take for you to get back on course.

The second reason it's important for you to evaluate your progress is that it enables you to focus on the intermediate successes you have. It gives you an opportunity to pat yourself on the back as you're progressing. Think of it this way. Have you ever made a "to do" list of what you want to accomplish during any given day? Each time you accomplish one of the tasks, you cross it off the list. That feels good, doesn't it. In essence what you're doing here is evaluating your progress. You are checking to make sure you're on course for what you set out to accomplish during that day.

You'll notice that the emphasis here is on what you have accomplished, not what is still on your list of things to do. Unfortunately, our tendency is to look at what's left to do, not what we have already accomplished. Looking at what remains to be done can be a burden and can get you down after a while. While evaluating your progress, keep that focus balanced. Recognize where you need to correct your course, but also acknowledge your successes. Back to our sailboat example: okay, so you were a little off course; but that doesn't negate the fact that you stocked the galley wisely, tested the fishing gear, stowed the proper emergency equipment, found the best maps and charts, and even remembered the first mate's favorite brand of soda. Acknowledging successful intermediate steps toward your goals results in encouragement to continue on your course, and in higher self-esteem.

Evaluating—assessing where you are and how close you are to your goal— takes time, it takes concentration, and it takes a concerted effort to look closely and honestly at your progress. This will help you see even the smallest success or most minor correction necessary toward fulfilling your dreams. Another essential ingredient of evaluation is an open mind, with a willingness to accept the reality your evaluation reveals.

RECAP: Evaluation means checking your progress, making corrections and recognizing your intermediate successes.

QUESTIONS FOR EVALUATING:

Can I change my goal?

Goals are not cast in cement...you didn't have them bronzed or etched in marble. One of the purposes of evaluation is to get an honest reading of exactly what you're doing, how you're doing it, and how you're progressing. It certainly follows that, if evaluation reveals something doesn't seem to be working, goals *can* be changed or modified. That doesn't mean that if your goal is a little bit out of reach or is tougher to reach than you expected, that you immediately change it or give it up altogether.

The point is that you need to be flexible, but realistic. Don't let your self-talk push you further down the Self-Esteem Slide. Grab that guardrail—*stop*—and analyze your situation. (We said analyze, not *over* analyze—you know how that trap works.) You might find yourself saying something like, "Oh, oh. This is more than I bargained for. I need to adjust." So adjust, and congratulate yourself for your foresight.

Another reason you might want to adjust your

goal is, it's too easy. Sometimes sights are too short, and goals are reached with no stretch whatsoever. When your goals are too easy, and aren't sufficiently challenging, you know in your heart you're not improving yourself and reaching your potential. It's like eating marshmallows: it's fun for a while, and gives you a little sugar high, but there's no substance, no nourishment, and afterward you're still hungry for some real food to sink your teeth into. Toying with yourself and setting goals too low can actually backfire and result in your feeling worse about yourself because of your deception. Enjoy the stretch for your goals like you savor the success of meeting them.

You may also decide to change your goal if you realize, after learning more about it, that it is not for you. We know a successful business woman who for years thought about going to law school. She wasn't completely sure she wanted to be a lawyer, but the idea had a lot of appeal to her. She finally enrolled in law school and even worked part-time for an attorney. After investing a little more than a year she realized that being a lawyer was not for her, and she quit law school and returned to her previous profession. People asked her, "Isn't it too bad that you wasted a whole year of your life?" She responded to the contrary. She felt that, first of all, the knowledge she obtained while in law school was knowledge she would be able to use for the rest of her life. She also felt it was valuable because now she would no longer have to wonder whether or not she should be an attorney, nor regret never trying to become one. Now she knew it was not what she wanted, and therefore could return to her former career with renewed vigor.

CHAPTER 9

Can I change my intermediate steps?

Of course you can. Intermediate steps are no different than your ultimate goal in this respect. They are, as we pointed out previously, little goals in and of themselves. In evaluating your progress, you need to ask if your intermediate steps are forcing you to REACH—not too much, but just enough. Are they sequenced properly? Are they frequent enough to allow you to periodically reward yourself? Are they keeping you on course toward your ultimate goal? If not, they should be changed.

Remember also, you needn't work ceaselessly, day in, day out, hammering away at the intermediate steps toward your goal. You shouldn't become a slave to your strategy. If things come up, or if you just need to lighten up and give yourself a break, you can pause for a bit without rendering all your effort useless. Promise yourself you'll regain momentum, get back to where you left off, and proceed with renewed enthusiasm and vitality. Then do just that.

Who can help me in my evaluating?

Again, as you did with networking in Chapter Seven, you must find people who are honest, who do care about you, and are not going to consciously or subconsciously sabotage your efforts. In some cases it may be the same people you sought out for advice and support, if you've been fortunate enough to develop a rapport with them. At any rate, determine who can give you suggestions and constructive criticisms in a caring but honest way.

A difficult aspect of this phase of evaluation is that it doesn't always feel good. For example, suppose your goal is to finish college in four years. You ask someone you trust to help you assess your progress, and he or she points out that since you're only taking six units this semester, it will be very hard to finish within your goal of four years. Now, it could be that you are only taking six units because you're working a lot of overtime at work—a good reason. If that is the case, don't fool yourself. Re-adjust your goal to a more realistic time line. By staying with the four year goal and working overtime, it is unlikely you will succeed in that time, and you may end up feeling like a failure. When reminded by your friend that six units per semester just won't get you there, you might get angry, hurt, or defensive. Those are natural emotions that you have the power to put aside. After all, what your friend says is true. It may be that you need to hear it from outside your own head, and adjust accordingly.

If you are honestly evaluating yourself, if you want to stay on course, succeed and ultimately enjoy high self-esteem, you will listen to your friend's or advisor's input and take it to heart. You may end up accepting and acting upon that input, or you may reject it. The important thing is that you listen to it and not get defensive.

We've all experienced the person who asks an opinion, then totally rejects it. Of course what they end up doing eventually is alienating their friends and advisors by wasting those people's valuable time and energy. (This is remindful of slogan on T-shirt: "Never try to teach a pig to sing. It wastes your time...and it annoys the pig." A bit coarse, but it does relay an honest message. Don't be like the singing teacher.) If you are going to seek advice, then listen. Others can be of great value in helping keep you on the road toward high self-esteem.

CHAPTER 9

Am I paying attention to my instincts?

We often have instincts, or what we call "gut feelings." It is important that you be aware of your instincts as you progress toward your goals. Somehow, as we grow up, many of us don't pay enough attention to, or even totally disregard, those gut feelings. We needn't go into the psychology of this behavior, but this can be a problem.

As an example, let's paint this little scene: a thirteen-year-old son is returning from his first out-of-state summer camp experience. Mom and dad are both there at the bus drop-off. Many times parents feel a need to react emotionally in particular circumstances, but somehow don't (or can't or won't) let themselves. This is one of those times. These people have missed their son very much, and are proud of his accomplishments. They both instinctively want to run up and give big hugs the moment he appears, but, sadly, they fall into the no-win situation of second-guessing...or intellectualizing: "If we run over and hug him, he'll probably be embarrassed...he's not a little kid any more...we don't want his new-found friends to think we're weird...or he's weird..." and so on.

The thought process that got in the way was fear of embarrassing the child. This fear was followed by self-talk which said, "I'd better not pursue this goal." The point here is twofold: the parents must be aware of getting away from their gut feelings and how that altered the course toward their goal. And secondly, the end result was, their son was deprived of the welcome-home greeting he may have needed and/or wanted. It may be that the decision to avoid the hug was correct and may have saved some embarrassment. Or it may have been incorrect, resulting in a hurt kid that didn't get a hug. But chances are good the initial instinct to give him a hug was right.

A very dynamic woman by the name of Anne Boe is a fine nationally known motivational speaker and has co-authored a book entitled *Is Your Net Working?* She makes a strong point about going with your gut reaction: "No one has to tell you when it's right." It's reminiscent of an advertising slogan of years gone by: "When it's right, you know it." Be aware of and trust your instincts. They are a valuable element in the evaluation process.

How am I feeling?

Don't ignore your *feelings*. They play a big role in monitoring and evaluating your progress. Not considering your feelings could result in self-deception and sabotage your efforts toward reaching your goals. Get to the root of your feelings; determine if they're based in reality, or if they're the result of negative self-talk. If they do stem from reality, acknowledge and pay attention to them. If they are the result of negative self-talk, then you need to take charge of your thoughts as we discussed in Chapter Two.

Some of the feelings you may experience as you evaluate your progress toward higher self-esteem are frustration, depression, elation, doubt, pride, anxiety, fear. Remember, these are all perfectly natural and occur—sometimes seemingly all at once!—whenever you are placing yourself on the line. Be aware of them, but be sure these feelings don't get the best of you. Don't allow the positive ones to sway you, nor the negative ones to get you down. You're in control.

Before we end this chapter, we have just a few words on

evaluating your results. Once you have attained your major goal, the first thing to do is to *celebrate!* Congratulate and reward yourself for a job well done.

So here you are enjoying your success. As we said, you should congratulate yourself, but then you should review how you got there. What did you do right? What strengths did you use to overcome the obstacles? These are important things for you to identify for two reasons: one is that in doing so, it gives you another opportunity to focus on the positive and feel good about yourself. The other reason to identify the strengths you used is, you are going to have more obstacles in the future. If you've identified the strengths you've used previously, you can use them again as needed. Put them in your quiver of arrows for use on your next target.

RECAP: Periodically ask yourself, "Are my actions getting me closer to or further from my goal?"

ACTION STEP FIVE: Evaluating

1. Rewrite your goal from Chapter Five.

2. Rewrite the intermediate steps you will take to accomplish your goal (from Chapter Six, Step 7) including the dates the intermediate steps were completed. (See next page.)

Intermediate Steps	Date to be completed	Actual date completed

3. Answer the following questions:
   a. Have you checked off the intermediate steps as you have accomplished them?
   b. Did you acknowledge and reward yourself for these successes?
   c. Have you sought and received input from others to help you in your evaluation?
   d. Are you focusing on your feelings and emotions and integrating them into your evaluation process?
   e. Did you accomplish your ultimate goal?
   f. Have you set new goals?
   g. Have you written them down?

Now, for completing the fifth Action Step toward toward achieving your self-esteem, congratulate and reward yourself. *Take pride in your achievement.*

CHAPTER 10

Maintenance

CHAPTER 10

Your diligence and perserverance have served you well, bringing you along to this, the final chapter. You should be proud of your efforts toward repairing or improving your self esteem. Now it's time to discuss how you can **maintain** high self-esteem throughout your life.

As with the automobile (that's put on so many miles as our most often-used example), proper **maintenance** will help you avoid future problems. We want you now to take everything you've learned from this book and incorporate it into your life: think the thoughts of a successful person, speak the language of a successful person, live the life of a successful person. No one maintains self-esteem by having a few successes and then resting on laurels, saying "Well, that's it. I feel good about myself."

It doesn't work that way. Maintenance is an ongoing process. Incorporate what you've learned here into your innermost thoughts. Own it, so the lessons become an automatic part of your daily life. Just like some of those negative thoughts that used to automatically be there, you can make this process a part of your very being, so that the automatic thoughts are positive, not negative.

The moment a car rolls off the assembly line is the

beginning of that vehicle's useful existence. Someone had an idea (as in **Envision**), then planned what it would look like, how it would work and how to get it built (as in **Strategize**). These ideas were checked and rechecked by talented experts for feasability and accepted, changed or adjusted as input was gathered (as in **Test**). When the planning was over, action was taken (as in **Engage**). Progress was measured (as in **Evaluate**), and finally the finished product is rolled out.

Certainly no car can be expected to run trouble-free, at peak performance, forever without some basic maintenance. Newer cars make maintenance a little easier by having electronic systems that give a signal when the car needs service. Maintaining a high level of self-esteem isn't that easy. There are no built-in flashing lights that tell us we are slipping back into our old habits.

You may roll your eyes...but the most universally identifiable example appropriate here is the often-discussed topic of weight loss. The fact is that most dieters regain lost weight within a two-year period following the end of their diet program. A new set of behaviors is adopted during the period of time they are on the diet, and while on the diet the dieter is highly conscious of the strategies and behaviors necessary for weight loss. But once an optimum weight is reached, these behaviors are forgotten, and old fattening habits are resumed. "Oh, I'll just have a donut or two. Look how thin I am! It won't matter." "I've just gained a few pounds; I'll lose them starting next Monday." Or "It's the holidays. I'll get back on my weight program after the first." Before you know it the pounds are on again, the old habits are back in place, and the self-esteem is sliding right down again—especially because you've let yourself down by backsliding...making a mockery of all your effort.

Weight maintenance requires the practice of good dietary habits *after the diet is over* and a desireable weight is achieved. Those good habits must become a part of you, must be automatic—a part of your everyday living. That's just how it is in the maintenance of high self-esteem.

The past five chapters have presented questions to help guide you through this process. In this chapter you'll find brief review statements and questions that will serve as a check list for keeping you on track, helping you maintain your high self-esteem. You'll also find affirmations to help you along the way.

Think of and use these statements and questions as you would your automobile maintenance checklist. Some of the items on this list you have to pay attention to each time you go through the process, some you don't. Read over the entire list anyway, just to be sure you don't miss anything.

• **The Four A's: ATTITUDE, ACTION, ACHIEVEMENT, and ACKNOWLEDGEMENT.** (Refer to Introduction.)
   1. Questions to ask yourself:
      A. What is my *attitude* today?
      B. Are my *actions* getting me closer to or further from my goals?
      C. Are my actions leading to *achievements?*
      D. How have I *acknowledged* my achievements?

• **Self-esteem is based on three areas of personal awareness.** (Refer to Chapter One.) They are:
   1. Accepting my own worth and importance.
      A. Affirmation: I am a person of worth and

importance. I feel good about myself.
2. Accountability for myself.
   A. Affirmation: I am responsible for my actions and accept the consequences of my behavior.
3. Acting responsible toward others.
   A. Affirmation: I am aware that my actions affect others, and I act accordingly.

- **Self-esteem is a product of how we filter, evaluate, reject or accept input.** (Refer to Chapter Two.)
  1. Ask yourself these questions:
     A. Who am I listening to?
     B. Am I accepting input from people who care but have their own interests in mind which may affect their advice to me?
     C. Am I keeping in mind that I *choose* to accept or reject input?

- **Take charge of your thoughts.** (Refer to Chapters Two and Three.)
  1. Remember that thoughts are real and have an impact on your behavior.
  2. *You control your thoughts.*
     A. Affirmation: I am in total control of my thoughts.

- **Are you remembering to test your strategies?** (Refer to Chapter Seven.)
  1. Don't try to do it alone—get help and advice from others.
  2. Are the people I'm networking with positive influences on me?

CHAPTER 10

- Self-esteem is built from a step-by-step progression of successes that result from your actions. (Refer to Chapters One and Six)
  1. Am I being careful to take appropriate steps; not too large and not too small?
  2. Am I rewarding myself for each small success I have on the way to my goals?

- To repair or maintain self-esteem, remember to focus continually on your strengths. (Chapters Two, Six and Nine)
  1. Practice updating your "I like this about me" list. As your self-esteem improves, your "I like me" list should be easier to develop and gradually get longer.
  2. Practice rewriting this list at least once a month or even more often.

- Continue to hold a conversation with yourself. (Refer to Chapter Five.)
  1. Practice asking questions and answering them as if you were two people. (Do not do this aloud on the bus.)

- Focus your thinking on now and the future. Yesterday is gone. (Refer to Chapter Two.)
  1. Questions to ask yourself:
     A. Where am I now?
     B. Where am I going?
     C. How am I planning to get there?

- Watch your language! Avoid negative self-talk. (Refer to Chapters Two, Three and Eight.)
  1. Pay attention to your self-talk; if you catch any negativity, push it aside.

2. Replace negativity with something positive.
3. You won't always feel great about yourself, but even (or especially) in your down times, refuse to give in to negative self-talk.

• **Avoid the dreaded "Self-Esteem Slide."** (Refer to Chapter Three.)
  1. Believe in yourself!
  2. Always keep trying—never give up!
  3. Keep a clear and honest picture of your strengths.
  4. Take action!
  5. Acknowledge your achievements.

• **Are you dreaming new dreams?** (Refer to Chapter Five.)
  1. Remember, this is an ongoing process. Allow yourself the challenge and the pleasure of continually creating new dreams and goals.

EPILOGUE

We began this book by stating our intentions to make this book short and to the point. We realize that there were many places where we could have expanded and discussed the theory behind some of the points we made. We are asking you again to accept our premise that it is not necessary to know the theories in order to repair or maintain your self-esteem. If you are interested in learning more of the different theories, fine. There are many good books to assist you in this endeavor; however, if your goal is to repair your self-esteem and maintain it at a high level, we believe all you need is in this book.

The reality is that you have successes every day without even planning them. What you must learn to do is recognize the unplanned as well as the planned successes and use all of them to enhance your self-esteem. Often it is just a matter of how you look at things—your perception.

Rex recalls the honor of speaking at a high school graduation. "Before the ceremony I heard a couple of the kids say, 'What's the big deal? It's only a high school diploma.' It's too bad these kids would feel that way, because they had achieved a significant goal, and they were denying themselves the satisfaction of acknowledging it."

That is an example of what we mean when we say, "It's all in how you look at it." Graduating from high school is an important achievement. Don't diminish this or any other achievement; use them as springboards to future achievements.

Remember way back in the introduction when we discussed the **Four A's?** By working through this book, you have developed a positive **Attitude** toward yourself and taken appropriate **Action**, hopefully leading to **Achievements.** Now **Acknowledge** them. Build on them, and the high level of self-esteem you'll feel will keep those doors to great heights of happiness and contentment wide open throughout your life.

B. David Brooks, Ph.D.

Rex K. Dalby, M.S.

A nationally recognized authority on self-esteem and personal responsibility, Dr. B. David Brooks has been the focus of many reports aired on network news broadcasts and programs such as 20/20, NBC's Today Show and ABC's The American Agenda.

Appointed by Gov. Deukmejian to California's Task Force to Promote Self-Esteem and Personal and Social Responsibility, David Brooks is the author of educational programs used throughout the country, including *How to be Successful in Less Than Ten Minutes a Day — The Twelve Steps to Success,* as well as numerous books and articles.

Dr. Brooks is president of The Thomas Jefferson Center in Pasadena, California. The Center works with schools to promote personal responsibility through systematic instruction and staff training.

Rex Dalby is widely acclaimed as an educator, speaker, counselor and consultant for schools as well as business and government organizations. He has trained thousands of adults and children nationally in self-esteem and personal and social responsibility, effective communication skills, and suicide and substance abuse prevention.

Mr. Dalby is co-producer and co-host of videos including *Self-Esteem: Building a Strong Foundation for your Child,* and audio tape programs such as *Parenting for the 21st Century.*

A respected expert as well as a highly effective communicator, Rex Dalby is a frequent guest on radio and television talk shows around the country. He is president of Rex K. Dalby & Associates, Huntington Beach, California.